The Impact of Social Media on Teenage Girls' Mental Health

Exploring the Influence of Online Platforms on the Wellbeing of Young Women

Mary L. Edwards

Table of Contents

Chapter 8 Maintaining Progress Long-Term Strategies for Sustaining Mental Wellness and Healthy Social Media Use

Conclusion

Introduction

A Journey to Mental Wellness and Social Media

As I sit here, reflecting on the journey that has brought me to this moment, I am filled with a mix of emotions. There is a sense of relief, knowing that I have finally found the courage to share my story and the struggles I have faced. There is also a sense of vulnerability, knowing that I am about to bare my soul to the world. But most of all, there is a sense of hope. Hope that by sharing my story, I can help others who may be struggling with the same issues.

As a woman, I have always been taught to be strong, to be resilient, and to never show weakness. But the truth is, we are not invincible. We are human beings, prone to the same emotions and struggles as anyone else. And yet, we are often expected to put on a brave face and carry on, even when our mental health is suffering. I remember the first time I felt the weight of mental health struggles. I was in my early twenties, and I had just gone through a difficult breakup. I felt lost, alone, and like I was drowning in a sea of emotions. I didn't know how to cope, and I didn't know where to turn. I felt like I was the only one who was struggling, like I was the only one who was broken.

But as I looked around, I realized that I was not alone. I saw women of all ages and backgrounds, struggling with the same issues. I saw women who were struggling to balance work and family life, women who were struggling with body image and self-esteem, and women who were struggling to find their place in the world.

And yet, despite the prevalence of mental health struggles, there is still a stigma surrounding mental illness. There is still a sense that mental health is something to be ashamed of, something that is a sign of weakness. But the truth is, mental health is not something to be ashamed of. It is something to be celebrated, something to be prioritized. As I began to share my story with others, I realized that I was not alone. I realized that there were countless women who were struggling with the same issues, and who were desperate for support and guidance. And that is why I wrote this book. I wrote it to help women find the support and guidance they need to navigate the challenges of mental health and social media. In the following pages, I will share my own story of struggle and resilience. I will share the strategies and techniques that have helped me to manage my mental health, and the lessons I have learned along the way. I will also share the stories of other women who have faced similar challenges, and who have found the strength to overcome them. My hope is that this book will be a source of comfort and support for women who are struggling with mental health issues. My hope is that it will be a reminder that they are not alone, and that they are not weak. My hope is that it will be a guide to help them find the strength and resilience they need to overcome their struggles and live happy, healthy lives.

As I look back on my journey, I am reminded of the power of vulnerability and the importance of community. I am reminded that we are not alone in our struggles, and that we are stronger together. And I am reminded that by sharing our stories and supporting one another, we can overcome even the most daunting challenges. So I invite you to join me on this journey. Let us walk together, hand in hand, as we navigate the complexities of mental health and social media. Let us support one another, and let us celebrate our strength and resilience. Together, we can overcome anything.

Why This Book Matters

In today's fast-paced and ever-changing world, mental health has become a pressing concern for individuals of all ages and backgrounds. However, women, in particular, face unique challenges that can significantly impact their mental well-being. This book, "Empowering Women: A Journey to Mental Wellness and Social Media," aims to address these challenges and provide a comprehensive guide to help women navigate the complexities of mental health and social media.

The importance of mental health cannot be overstated. Mental health affects every aspect of a person's life, from relationships and work to overall well-being and happiness. Unfortunately, women are disproportionately affected by mental health issues, with higher rates of depression, anxiety, and post-traumatic stress disorder (PTSD) compared to men. The consequences of poor mental health can be severe, leading to decreased productivity, strained relationships, and even physical health problems.

Understanding the Importance of Mental Health for Women

Women's mental health is often influenced by a combination of biological, psychological, and social factors. Hormonal changes during menstruation, pregnancy, and menopause can contribute to mood swings and emotional instability. Additionally, societal expectations and gender roles can create pressure to conform to traditional norms, leading to feelings of inadequacy and low self-esteem.

Furthermore, women are more likely to experience trauma and stress due to their increased exposure to domestic violence, sexual harassment, and other forms of gender-based violence. These experiences can have long-lasting effects on mental health, making it essential for women to have access to resources and support.

How Social Media Affects Mental Health

Social media has become an integral part of modern life, with billions of people worldwide using platforms like Facebook, Instagram, and Twitter.

While social media can be a powerful tool for connection and self-expression, it also has a significant impact on mental health.

Social media can contribute to feelings of inadequacy and low self-esteem by presenting unrealistic beauty and lifestyle standards. The constant stream of curated content can create unrealistic expectations, leading to feelings of disappointment and dissatisfaction with one's own life. Moreover, social media can exacerbate mental health issues by providing a platform for cyberbullying, online harassment, and the spread of misinformation. The constant notifications and updates can also lead to increased stress and anxiety, making it difficult for individuals to disconnect and relax.

The Purpose of This Book: Empowering Women Through Mental Wellness and Social Media

This book aims to empower women by providing a comprehensive guide to mental wellness and social media. The purpose is to educate women on the importance of mental health, the impact of social media on mental health, and strategies for maintaining a healthy balance between the two.

The book is divided into five parts, each focusing on a specific aspect of mental wellness and social media. Part One explores the importance of mental health for women, while Part Two examines the role of social media in shaping mental health. Part Three provides strategies for building resilience and coping with stress and anxiety, while Part Four offers practical tips for managing social media use. Finally, Part Five presents a 30-day plan for improving mental wellness and maintaining a healthy social media presence. Throughout the book, readers will find exercises, takeaways, and real-life examples to help them apply the concepts to their own lives. The book also includes appendices with additional resources, a glossary of mental health terms, and common mental health myths debunked.

"Empowering Women: A Journey to Mental Wellness and Social Media" is a vital resource for women seeking to improve their mental health and manage their social media use effectively. By understanding the importance of mental health, the impact of social media, and strategies for maintaining a healthy balance, women can take control of their mental wellness and live happier, healthier lives.

Chapter 1

Understanding Mental Health

The Urgent Problem of Mental Health in Women

Mental health is a critical issue that affects millions of individuals worldwide, but it manifests differently and often more acutely in women due to a combination of biological, social, and cultural factors. Understanding the specific challenges women face in terms of mental health requires a deep dive into the historical context, the myriad of influences affecting their well-being, and the necessary steps to address these challenges effectively. This chapter will explore the urgent nature of mental health issues in women, examining the legacy of silence and stigma, the intricate web of factors impacting their lives, and the compelling need for a multifaceted approach to address these concerns.

The Historical Context: A Legacy of Silence and Stigma

The history of mental health in women is a narrative marked by silence and stigma, deeply rooted in societal norms and expectations. Historically, mental health has been a topic shrouded in taboo, and for women, this was compounded by rigid gender roles that defined their identities primarily as caregivers and homemakers.

The Early Silence

In many ancient societies, mental illness was often attributed to supernatural causes or moral failings. Women, particularly those who exhibited symptoms of mental distress, were frequently labeled as hysterical or possessed. The term "hysteria" itself derives from the Greek word for uterus, reflecting the longstanding association between women's reproductive functions and their mental health. This medicalization of women's emotions and behaviors as "hysteria" persisted into the 19th century, reinforcing the notion that women were inherently prone to mental instability.

Victorian Era and Beyond

During the Victorian era, societal expectations confined women to domestic spheres, where their roles were strictly defined as wives and mothers. Mental health issues were rarely discussed openly, and women who struggled with their mental health were often subjected to harsh treatments, including institutionalization and various forms of restraint. These treatments were based on the prevailing belief that women's mental health issues were rooted in their biological inferiority and emotional fragility. The era's moral and social codes discouraged women from expressing dissatisfaction or seeking help, thereby perpetuating a culture of silence and suppression.

The 20th Century: Slow Progress

The 20th century saw some progress in the understanding of mental health, but women continued to face significant barriers. The rise of psychoanalysis and later, psychiatric medication, offered new insights and treatments for mental health disorders. However, women's mental health issues were still often misunderstood or minimized. The feminist movement of the 1960s and 1970s began to challenge these norms, advocating for greater recognition of women's experiences and their right to mental health care. Yet, stigma and gender bias in mental health care persisted, influencing both the diagnosis and treatment of women's mental health conditions.

Contemporary Challenges

In contemporary society, while there has been substantial progress in recognizing and treating mental health issues, women still face unique challenges. The legacy of historical stigma lingers, influencing how women perceive and access mental health care. Modern societal pressures, including the expectation to balance professional careers with familial responsibilities, add to the stress experienced by women. Although there is a greater understanding of mental health today, women often struggle with the internalized belief that they must cope silently or that their mental health issues are secondary to their other roles and responsibilities.

The Impact on Women's Lives: A Web of Factors

Mental health issues profoundly affect women's lives, influencing their relationships, professional endeavors, and overall quality of life. This impact is complex and multifaceted, shaped by an intricate interplay of biological, social, economic, cultural, and personal factors.

Biological Factors

Hormonal Changes: Women experience significant hormonal fluctuations throughout their lives, including during menstruation, pregnancy, postpartum periods, and menopause. These hormonal changes can influence mood and emotional stability. Premenstrual Dysphoric Disorder (PMDD), for instance, is a severe form of premenstrual syndrome that affects a small percentage of women, causing intense emotional and physical symptoms. Similarly, postpartum depression affects many new mothers, manifesting as severe depression and anxiety after childbirth. Menopausal transition also brings about hormonal changes that can exacerbate mood disorders.

Genetic Predispositions: Research indicates that certain mental health conditions, such as depression and anxiety, may have a genetic component. Women with a family history of these disorders may be more susceptible to experiencing similar issues. Genetic factors, combined with environmental stressors, can create a predisposition to mental health challenges that require careful management and support.

Biological Stress Response: Women often exhibit a different biological response to stress compared to men. The hypothalamic-pituitary-adrenal (HPA) axis, which regulates stress response, may function differently in women, potentially leading to heightened vulnerability to stress-related disorders such as anxiety and depression. This difference underscores the importance of gender-sensitive approaches to understanding and treating stress-related mental health issues in women.

Social and Economic Factors

Economic Inequities: Women are disproportionately affected by economic hardships. Globally, women are more likely than men to live in poverty, have limited access to education, and face employment discrimination. These economic disparities limit their ability to access mental health care and other essential services. Financial stress is a significant factor contributing to mental health issues, creating a cycle where economic instability exacerbates mental health challenges, which in turn hinders economic opportunities and stability.

Gender-Based Violence: Women are at a higher risk of experiencing gender-based violence, including domestic abuse, sexual assault, and harassment. These traumatic experiences can have severe and long-lasting impacts on mental health, leading to conditions such as PTSD, depression, and anxiety. The fear and trauma associated with violence often go unaddressed due to social stigma, lack of support, and inadequate legal protections, further entrenching mental health issues.

Caregiving Responsibilities: Women frequently shoulder a disproportionate share of caregiving responsibilities, whether for children, elderly family members, or partners. This caregiving role, while fulfilling for many, can also be a significant source of stress and exhaustion. The emotional and physical demands of caregiving can contribute to burnout and mental health deterioration, particularly when women lack adequate support and resources to manage these responsibilities effectively.

Cultural and Societal Factors

Societal Expectations: Cultural norms often dictate that women should be nurturing, self-sacrificing, and resilient in the face of adversity. These expectations can create intense pressure to conform to idealized roles as perfect mothers, wives, and professionals. When women struggle to meet these expectations, they may experience feelings of guilt, shame, and inadequacy, which can contribute to mental health issues. The societal expectation to maintain a façade of competence and composure, even when experiencing distress, further complicates women's ability to seek help.

Stigma and Silence: Despite advances in understanding mental health, stigma remains a powerful barrier to seeking help. Women may fear judgment or discrimination if they disclose their mental health struggles, leading them to cope in silence. This stigma is often compounded by cultural attitudes that dismiss or minimize women's mental health issues, reinforcing the notion that such issues are a sign of weakness or personal failing.

Representation and Media: Media representations of women often perpetuate unrealistic standards of beauty, success, and happiness. These portrayals can influence women's self-esteem and body image, contributing to mental health challenges such as eating disorders and depression. The pressure to conform to idealized images and lifestyles, as depicted in media, can exacerbate feelings of inadequacy and anxiety, particularly when women compare themselves unfavorably to these unattainable standards.

Personal Factors

Trauma and Abuse: Personal experiences of trauma and abuse are significant factors in the mental health of women. Survivors of physical, emotional, or sexual abuse often face long-term psychological effects, including depression, anxiety, and PTSD. The process of healing from trauma is complex and requires access to supportive, trauma-informed care. Many women, however, may struggle to find or afford the necessary resources to address the deep-seated impacts of their experiences.

Loss and Grief: Women who experience significant losses, such as the death of a loved one, a miscarriage, or divorce, often face profound grief and emotional distress. These experiences can trigger or exacerbate mental health issues, requiring sensitive and appropriate support to navigate the grieving process and rebuild emotional well-being.

Interpersonal Relationships: The quality of interpersonal relationships plays a crucial role in women's mental health. Supportive relationships can provide emotional sustenance and resilience, while toxic or abusive relationships can be sources of significant stress and anxiety. Women who lack a strong support network may feel isolated and unsupported, further compounding their mental health challenges.

The Need for Action: Breaking the Silence and Stigma

Addressing the urgent problem of mental health in women requires a concerted effort to break the silence and stigma that have historically surrounded this issue. A multifaceted approach is essential to create meaningful change and improve mental health outcomes for women.

Increased Awareness

Public Education Campaigns: Raising awareness about the unique mental health challenges faced by women is crucial for fostering a more supportive environment. Public education campaigns can play a pivotal role in normalizing discussions about mental health and encouraging women to seek help. These campaigns should aim to dismantle stereotypes, educate about the signs and symptoms of mental health issues, and highlight the importance of early intervention.

Media Representation: Media has a powerful influence on societal attitudes and can be leveraged to promote positive messages about women's mental health. Accurate and compassionate portrayals of women dealing with mental health issues can reduce stigma and encourage empathy. Media platforms can also be used to share stories of resilience and recovery, providing hope and inspiration to women struggling with their mental health.

Community Engagement: Engaging communities in conversations about mental health can help to break down barriers and foster a culture of openness and support. Community-based initiatives, such as workshops, support groups, and public forums, can provide safe spaces for women to discuss their experiences, share resources, and seek support. Involving local organizations, religious institutions, and community leaders can enhance outreach and promote mental health literacy at the grassroots level.

Access to Care

Affordable and Accessible Services: Ensuring that mental health services are affordable and accessible to all women is a critical step in addressing mental health disparities. This includes expanding public health insurance coverage for mental health services, providing subsidies or sliding scale fees, and supporting community mental health centers that offer low-cost or free services.

Telehealth options should be expanded to reach women in remote or underserved areas, providing them with the flexibility to access care regardless of location. Culturally Sensitive Care: Mental health services must be culturally sensitive and attuned to the diverse backgrounds of women. This involves training healthcare providers to understand and respect cultural differences in mental health perceptions and practices, and to provide care that is inclusive and respectful of women's cultural contexts. Providing care in multiple languages and ensuring that services are accessible to women of all backgrounds can help reduce barriers to seeking help.

Integrated Care Models: Integrating mental health services with primary care can improve access and reduce stigma. Women are more likely to seek mental health support if it is provided within the context of their routine healthcare. Integrated care models allow for the early identification and treatment of mental health issues, and can provide a more holistic approach to health by addressing both physical and mental health needs simultaneously.

Workplace and Academic Support: Employers and educational institutions should play a role in supporting women's mental health by offering mental health resources, creating supportive policies, and fostering environments that prioritize well-being. This includes providing employee assistance programs (EAPs), mental health days, flexible work arrangements, and mental health education and training for staff and students.

Policy Change

Legislative Advocacy: Advocacy for policy changes that address the specific mental health needs of women is essential. This includes advocating for laws that protect women's mental health rights, fund research into women's mental health issues, and ensure parity between mental health and physical health care in insurance coverage. Policies should also address social determinants of health, such as economic support, protections against gender-based violence, and access to safe housing and employment opportunities.

Research and Funding: Increasing funding for research on women's mental health can help to better understand the unique challenges they face and develop targeted interventions. Research should focus on the biological, social, and cultural factors that influence women's mental health, as well as the effectiveness of different treatment approaches. Funding should also support the development of innovative programs and services that address the specific needs of women.

Intersectional Approaches: Policies and programs should adopt an intersectional approach that recognizes the diverse experiences of women. This includes considering factors such as race, ethnicity, socioeconomic status, sexual orientation, disability, and immigration status, and ensuring that mental health services are inclusive and equitable for all women. Intersectional approaches can help to identify and address the unique barriers faced by different groups of women, promoting more effective and inclusive mental health care.

Community Support

Building Support Networks: Creating and strengthening support networks is crucial for women's mental health. Community support groups, peer networks, and online forums can provide women with a sense of belonging, validation, and practical advice. These networks can help women to feel less isolated and more connected, and can provide a platform for sharing experiences and resources.

Peer Support Programs: Peer support programs, where women who have experienced mental health challenges offer support to others going through similar issues, can be highly effective. These programs provide a sense of understanding and empathy that can be invaluable in the recovery process. Training and empowering women to become peer supporters can also enhance their own sense of purpose and resilience.

Educational and Supportive Environments: Creating educational and supportive environments that promote mental health awareness and well-being can have a significant impact. This includes schools, workplaces, and community centers that offer mental health education, promote positive coping strategies, and provide resources and referrals to mental health services. Educational programs should focus on building resilience, reducing stigma, and encouraging help-seeking behaviors.

Family and Caregiver Support: Supporting the mental health of women also involves providing support to their families and caregivers. Family education programs can help relatives to understand mental health issues and learn how to provide effective support. Caregiver support groups and resources can help those who are caring for women with mental health issues to manage their own stress and well-being.

Women face a unique and urgent set of mental health challenges shaped by a complex interplay of historical, biological, social, economic, cultural, and personal factors. Recognizing and addressing these challenges is critical for improving mental health outcomes for women.

Breaking the silence and stigma that have historically surrounded women's mental health requires a multifaceted approach that includes increasing awareness, improving access to care, advocating for policy change, and building supportive communities. By raising public awareness and normalizing discussions about women's mental health, we can reduce stigma and encourage more women to seek help. Ensuring that mental health services are affordable, accessible, and culturally sensitive can provide women with the support they need to address their mental health challenges.

Advocating for policy changes that protect women's mental health rights and address social determinants of health can promote equity and improve access to care. Building supportive communities that foster open dialogue and provide peer support can empower women to prioritize their mental health and seek help when needed. By working together to address the urgent problem of mental health in women, we can create a more supportive and equitable society that promotes mental health and well-being for all women, enabling them to lead healthier, more fulfilling lives.

This comprehensive approach will help to dismantle the legacy of silence and stigma that has long overshadowed women's mental health, paving the way for a future where mental health care is accessible, inclusive, and effective for all women.

Chapter 2

The Role of Social Media

Social media has revolutionized the way we communicate, connect, and consume information. With platforms like Facebook, Instagram, Twitter, TikTok, and others, the digital landscape has become a central part of modern life. While social media offers many benefits, such as connecting with loved ones, discovering communities, and sharing experiences, it also poses significant challenges, especially concerning mental health. In this section, we will explore the impact of social media on mental health, how it influences body image and self-esteem, and the darker aspects, including cyberbullying and online harassment.

The Impact of Social Media on Mental Health

The relationship between social media and mental health is complex and multifaceted. Social media can enhance communication and provide support networks, yet it can also contribute to feelings of inadequacy, anxiety, and depression. Understanding this dual nature requires examining how social media affects various aspects of mental well-being.

Positive Effects of Social Media

Connection and Community: Social media can foster a sense of connection and belonging by allowing individuals to maintain relationships across distances, reconnect with old friends, and find communities of like-minded individuals. For many, especially those who feel isolated in their offline lives, social media provides a platform to share experiences, seek support, and form meaningful connections.

Information and Awareness: Social media serves as a powerful tool for spreading information and raising awareness about mental health issues. Campaigns, support groups, and educational content on platforms like Instagram and Twitter have helped reduce stigma and promote mental health literacy. Access to mental health resources and communities can empower individuals to seek help and support.

Creative Expression: For some, social media offers an outlet for creativity and self-expression. Platforms like TikTok and Instagram provide opportunities to share art, music, writing, and personal stories, which can be therapeutic and contribute to a sense of identity and purpose.

Comparison and Envy: Social media often presents curated, idealized versions of life. The constant exposure to seemingly perfect images and lifestyles can lead to unhealthy comparisons. Users may feel inadequate or envious when comparing their own lives to the highlight reels of others, contributing to feelings of anxiety, depression, and low self-esteem.

Fear of Missing Out (FOMO): The fear of missing out is a common phenomenon exacerbated by social media. Seeing friends and acquaintances participate in events, travel, or enjoy experiences can create a sense of exclusion or inadequacy. FOMO can lead to compulsive checking of social media and contribute to anxiety and dissatisfaction.

Sleep Disruption: Excessive use of social media, particularly before bedtime, can disrupt sleep patterns. The blue light emitted by screens affects the production of melatonin, a hormone that regulates sleep. Additionally, engaging in emotionally charged interactions or consuming distressing content late at night can interfere with the ability to relax and fall asleep, impacting overall mental health.

Addiction and Dependency: The design of social media platforms encourages frequent use through notifications, likes, and shares, which can create a dependency. The constant need for validation and the dopamine release associated with social media interactions can lead to addictive behaviors. This dependency can detract from real-life interactions and responsibilities, contributing to social isolation and mental health issues.

Echo Chambers and Polarization: Social media algorithms often promote content that aligns with users' existing beliefs, creating echo chambers. This can reinforce negative thoughts and behaviors, particularly in communities that propagate harmful ideologies or misinformation. Exposure to polarized or hostile content can increase stress, anxiety, and a sense of division, impacting mental well-being.

How Social Media Influences Body Image and Self-Esteem

Body image and self-esteem are closely intertwined with mental health, and social media plays a significant role in shaping perceptions of oneself. Platforms that emphasize visual content, such as Instagram and TikTok, can influence how individuals perceive their bodies and self-worth. This chapter explores the mechanisms through which social media affects body image and self-esteem, highlighting both positive and negative influences.

The Role of Visual Content

Curated Perfection: Social media platforms often showcase idealized and heavily edited images. Filters, photo editing tools, and strategic posing create an unattainable standard of beauty that can distort users' perceptions of reality. This constant exposure to perfected images can lead to body dissatisfaction and low self-esteem, particularly among young women and adolescents who are more susceptible to societal pressures regarding appearance.

Influencers and Celebrities: Influencers and celebrities often set trends in beauty, fashion, and lifestyle. Their posts can perpetuate unrealistic beauty standards, such as slim bodies, flawless skin, and luxurious lifestyles. Followers may internalize these standards, leading to a sense of inadequacy or failure when they cannot achieve the same appearance or lifestyle. The phenomenon of "influencer culture" contributes to a cycle of comparison and self-criticism.

Fitspiration and Diet Culture: Movements like "fitspiration" and diet culture on social media promote specific body ideals and fitness routines. While they can motivate healthy behaviors, they often emphasize extreme or unsustainable practices. The pressure to conform to these ideals can lead to disordered eating, exercise addiction, and negative body image. Users may feel compelled to compare their bodies to those of fitness influencers, fostering unhealthy attitudes towards food and exercise.

Body Positivity and Acceptance: On the positive side, social media has also given rise to the body positivity and acceptance movements. These movements advocate for the acceptance of diverse body types and challenge traditional beauty standards. By promoting messages of self-love and body acceptance, these communities provide support for individuals struggling with body image issues. They offer an alternative narrative that celebrates diversity and encourages users to embrace their natural appearance.

The Impact on Self-Esteem

Validation and Feedback: Social media interactions, such as likes, comments, and shares, can influence self-esteem. Positive feedback can boost self-esteem and confidence, while negative comments or lack of engagement can have the opposite effect. The pursuit of social validation through social media can create a dependency on external approval, undermining intrinsic self-worth.

Cyberbullying and Criticism: Negative feedback and cyberbullying are significant threats to self-esteem. Hurtful comments, body shaming, and harassment can severely impact mental health, leading to anxiety, depression, and decreased self-esteem. The anonymity of online interactions often emboldens individuals to engage in aggressive or critical behavior, further exacerbating the issue.

Self-Perception and Identity: Social media can shape how individuals perceive themselves and construct their identities. The pressure to present a curated, positive image online can lead to discrepancies between one's online persona and real-life self. This dissonance can contribute to feelings of inauthenticity and self-doubt, impacting overall self-esteem.

Comparison and Self-Worth: The pervasive nature of social comparison on social media can erode self-esteem. Users frequently compare their bodies, lifestyles, and achievements to those of others, often coming up short against idealized portrayals. This constant comparison can lead to negative self-evaluation and diminished self-worth, particularly when individuals feel they cannot measure up to the standards set by their peers or influencers.

Chapter 3

The Dark Side of Social Media

Cyberbullying and Online Harassment

While social media has the potential to connect and empower individuals, it also harbors a darker side characterized by cyberbullying and online harassment. These negative aspects of social media can have profound effects on mental health, leading to anxiety, depression, and even suicidal ideation. This chapter explores the prevalence, impact, and strategies for addressing cyberbullying and online harassment.

Prevalence of Cyberbullying and Online Harassment

Widespread Issue: Cyberbullying and online harassment are pervasive problems affecting individuals across all demographics. Studies indicate that a significant proportion of social media users, particularly young people, have experienced some form of online harassment. This includes behaviors such as threatening messages, spreading rumors, impersonation, and public shaming.

Vulnerable Populations: Certain groups are more vulnerable to cyberbullying, including women, LGBTQ+ individuals, racial and ethnic minorities, and people with disabilities. Women, in particular, are often targeted with gender-based harassment, including sexual harassment and threats of violence. These experiences can be especially damaging to mental health and well-being.

Platforms and Anonymity: The anonymity provided by many social media platforms can embolden perpetrators of cyberbullying. Platforms that allow anonymous interactions or provide minimal oversight can become breeding grounds for harassment. The lack of accountability and the ability to hide behind a screen can lead to more aggressive and harmful behaviors.

Impact on Mental Health

Anxiety and Depression: Victims of cyberbullying and online harassment often experience heightened levels of anxiety and depression. The constant fear of being targeted or the emotional toll of dealing with harassment can lead to significant psychological distress. This can manifest as symptoms such as panic attacks, social withdrawal, and persistent feelings of sadness or hopelessness.

Self-Esteem and Identity: Online harassment can severely impact self-esteem and personal identity. Victims may internalize the negative messages they receive, leading to diminished self-worth and a distorted sense of identity. The relentless nature of cyberbullying can make it difficult for individuals to maintain a positive self-image or to feel safe and valued.

Isolation and Loneliness: The experience of being bullied or harassed online can lead to social isolation. Victims may withdraw from social interactions, both online and offline, to avoid further harassment or out of fear of judgment. This isolation can exacerbate feelings of loneliness and further impact mental health.

Suicidal Ideation: In severe cases, cyberbullying and online harassment can contribute to suicidal thoughts and behaviors. The persistent nature of online harassment and the sense of helplessness it can create may lead some individuals to view suicide as their only escape. This underscores the critical need for effective interventions and support systems to protect individuals from the harmful effects of cyberbullying.

Addressing Cyberbullying and Online Harassment

Platform Responsibility: Social media platforms have a crucial role in mitigating cyberbullying and online harassment. They must implement robust policies and tools to identify, report, and respond to harassment. This includes automated systems for detecting harmful content, transparent reporting mechanisms, and effective moderation practices. Platforms should also enforce their community guidelines consistently, taking action against accounts that violate them to create safer environments for users.

Educational Programs: Education is key to preventing and addressing cyberbullying. Schools, parents, and community organizations should provide education on digital citizenship, online etiquette, and the risks associated with social media. Teaching young people about the impact of their online behavior and how to respond to cyberbullying can foster more responsible use of social media. Programs should also focus on building empathy and resilience to reduce the likelihood of individuals engaging in or being affected by cyberbullying.

Legal and Policy Measures: Governments and regulatory bodies need to enact and enforce laws that address online harassment and protect individuals from cyberbullying. Legal frameworks should provide clear definitions of cyberbullying, establish penalties for perpetrators, and offer avenues for victims to seek justice. Policies should also mandate that social media companies take proactive measures to prevent and respond to harassment on their platforms.

Support Services: Providing support for victims of cyberbullying is essential for mitigating its impact on mental health. This includes access to counseling, mental health services, and support groups that offer emotional support and practical advice. Helplines and online resources can provide immediate assistance and guidance for those experiencing online harassment. Support services should also focus on rebuilding self-esteem and resilience in victims to help them recover from their experiences.

Empowering Users: Individuals can take steps to protect themselves from cyberbullying and online harassment. This includes using privacy settings to control who can view their profiles and interact with them, blocking or reporting abusive users, and avoiding sharing personal information that could be used to target them. Encouraging users to document instances of harassment can also aid in reporting and seeking help. Empowering users with knowledge and tools can enhance their sense of control and safety online.

Promoting Positive Online Behavior: Encouraging positive online behavior and fostering supportive online communities can help counteract the negative aspects of social media. Campaigns that promote kindness, respect, and empathy online can create a more positive digital culture. Influencers and public figures can also play a role by modeling positive interactions and speaking out against cyberbullying.

Case Studies and Real-Life Impacts

Case Study 1: The Effects of Cyberbullying on Adolescents

Adolescents are particularly vulnerable to the effects of cyberbullying. A study conducted by the Pew Research Center found that 59% of U.S. teens have experienced some form of cyberbullying. The study highlighted that cyberbullying often occurs on social media platforms, where teens spend a significant amount of their time.

One notable case involved a teenager who faced relentless harassment on Instagram and Snapchat. The bullying included derogatory comments, spreading false rumors, and exclusion from social groups. The emotional toll led to severe anxiety, depression, and a decline in academic performance. The teen's experience underscores the importance of parental monitoring, school intervention, and accessible mental health resources to support adolescents dealing with cyberbullying.

Case Study 2: The Role of Support Networks in Overcoming Online Harassment

Support networks can play a crucial role in helping individuals cope with online harassment. In one case, a woman faced targeted harassment on Twitter due to her activism. The harassment included threats, doxxing, and coordinated attacks by trolls. The situation caused significant stress and fear for her safety.

However, the woman received support from online communities, friends, and mental health professionals. The support network provided emotional reassurance, practical advice on digital security, and assistance in reporting the harassment to Twitter and law enforcement. This case illustrates the importance of strong support systems and the power of community in helping individuals navigate and recover from online harassment.

The impact of social media on mental health is profound, encompassing both positive and negative dimensions. While social media can connect individuals, provide support, and offer opportunities for self-expression, it also poses risks to mental health through mechanisms such as comparison, fear of missing out, and dependency.

The influence of social media on body image and self-esteem is particularly significant, with platforms promoting idealized beauty standards that can lead to dissatisfaction and low self-worth. However, movements promoting body positivity and acceptance provide a counter-narrative, helping individuals embrace diversity and challenge harmful norms.

The dark side of social media, including cyberbullying and online harassment, presents serious threats to mental health. The prevalence of these issues and their impact on anxiety, depression, and self-esteem highlight the need for comprehensive strategies to address them. Social media platforms, educational institutions, legal frameworks, and support services all have roles to play in creating safer, more supportive digital environments.

Moving forward, it is essential to balance the benefits of social media with the need to protect mental health. By promoting positive online behavior, providing education and support, and holding platforms accountable, we can harness the potential of social media to enhance well-being while mitigating its risks. This balanced approach can help individuals navigate the digital landscape in ways that support their mental health and foster a more inclusive and compassionate online community.

Chapter 4
Strategies for Mental Wellness

Building Resilience: Strategies for Coping with Stress and Anxiety

Resilience is the capacity to recover from difficulties, adapt to change, and keep going in the face of adversity. It is not an innate trait but a set of skills that can be developed and strengthened over time. In a world filled with uncertainties and challenges, building resilience is essential for coping with stress and anxiety. This chapter explores various strategies for enhancing resilience, helping individuals navigate life's ups and downs with greater ease and confidence.

Understanding Resilience

Definition and Importance: Resilience is often described as the ability to bounce back from setbacks, maintain a positive outlook, and remain effective in the face of stress. It is crucial for mental health because it helps individuals manage stressors without succumbing to anxiety or depression. Resilient people are not immune to stress but are better equipped to handle it and recover more quickly.

Components of Resilience: Resilience comprises several key components:

Emotional Regulation: The ability to manage and respond to emotional experiences in a healthy way.

Optimism: A positive outlook on life and the future, which helps in viewing challenges as opportunities for growth.

Self-Efficacy: The belief in one's ability to influence events and outcomes in life, which fosters a sense of control and competence.

Social Support: Access to a network of supportive relationships that provide encouragement and assistance during tough times.

Adaptability: The capacity to adjust to new circumstances and modify one's approach to problem-solving as needed.

Strategies for Building Resilience

1. Developing a Growth Mindset

A growth mindset, as opposed to a fixed mindset, is the belief that abilities and intelligence can be developed through effort, learning, and persistence. This perspective encourages individuals to view challenges as opportunities to grow rather than insurmountable obstacles.

Embrace Challenges: Instead of avoiding difficult situations, see them as chances to learn and improve. This approach helps build confidence and problem-solving skills.

Learn from Criticism: Use feedback as a tool for growth. Constructive criticism can provide valuable insights into areas where improvement is possible.

Celebrate Effort, Not Just Success: Recognize and appreciate the hard work and effort put into achieving goals, regardless of the outcome. This fosters a sense of accomplishment and motivation to continue striving.

2. Strengthening Emotional Regulation

Emotional regulation involves managing one's emotions in a way that is appropriate and effective. It is crucial for maintaining resilience in the face of stress and adversity.

Practice Mindfulness: Mindfulness involves paying attention to the present moment without judgment. Techniques such as mindful breathing and meditation can help individuals become more aware of their emotions and respond to them in a balanced way.

Use Cognitive Reappraisal: This strategy involves changing the way one thinks about a situation to alter its emotional impact. For example, viewing a stressful event as a challenge rather than a threat can reduce anxiety and improve coping.

Develop Healthy Coping Mechanisms: Engaging in activities that promote relaxation and well-being, such as exercise, hobbies, or spending time with loved ones, can help manage stress and maintain emotional balance.

3. Enhancing Social Support

Having a strong support network is a critical aspect of resilience. Social connections provide emotional support, practical assistance, and a sense of belonging.

Build and Maintain Relationships: Invest time and effort in developing meaningful relationships with family, friends, and colleagues. Regular communication and shared activities can strengthen these bonds.

Seek Support When Needed: Don't hesitate to reach out for help during challenging times. Talking to someone you trust can provide perspective and emotional relief.

Contribute to Others: Offering support to others can also enhance your own resilience. Acts of kindness and helping behaviors can boost self-esteem and create a sense of purpose.

4. Fostering Optimism

Optimism involves maintaining a hopeful and positive outlook on life, even in the face of difficulties. It helps in viewing setbacks as temporary and manageable rather than overwhelming and permanent.

Practice Positive Thinking: Focus on positive aspects of your life and express gratitude for them. Keeping a gratitude journal can help reinforce this practice.

Set Realistic Goals: Break down large goals into smaller, achievable steps. Celebrate progress along the way to maintain motivation and a sense of accomplishment.

Visualize Success: Use visualization techniques to imagine positive outcomes for challenging situations. This can enhance confidence and readiness to tackle problems.

5. Building Self-Efficacy

Self-efficacy is the belief in your ability to succeed and make a difference in your life. It is essential for taking initiative and facing challenges with confidence.

Set Achievable Goals: Start with small, manageable tasks and gradually increase the difficulty. Success in smaller goals builds confidence to tackle larger challenges.
Learn New Skills: Continuously seek opportunities to acquire new skills and knowledge. This not only enhances competence but also fosters a sense of control over your life.
Reflect on Past Successes: Remind yourself of previous achievements and how you overcame challenges. This reinforces the belief in your ability to succeed again.

6. Cultivating Adaptability

Adaptability involves being flexible and open to change. It allows individuals to adjust their approach when faced with new or unexpected challenges.

Stay Open-Minded: Embrace change and be willing to explore different perspectives and solutions. Flexibility in thinking can lead to innovative ways of handling stress.

Develop Problem-Solving Skills: Enhance your ability to identify problems, evaluate options, and implement effective solutions. This reduces the perceived threat of new challenges.

Practice Stress Inoculation: Gradually expose yourself to stressors in a controlled way to build tolerance and improve coping skills. This technique helps in managing future stress more effectively.

The Power of Self-Care: Prioritizing Your Mental Health

Self-care involves taking intentional actions to maintain and improve one's physical, mental, and emotional well-being. It is a crucial component of mental health, helping individuals manage stress, prevent burnout, and enhance overall quality of life. This chapter delves into the importance of self-care, various self-care practices, and how to integrate them into daily routines to prioritize mental health effectively.

Understanding Self-Care

Definition and Importance: Self-care is any activity that individuals engage in to take care of their mental, emotional, and physical health. It is essential because it helps in managing stress, maintaining a healthy work-life balance, and preventing mental health issues. Effective self-care can improve mood, increase energy levels, and enhance resilience.

Barriers to Self-Care: Despite its importance, many people struggle to prioritize self-care due to various barriers, including:

Time Constraints: Busy schedules and numerous responsibilities can make it difficult to find time for self-care activities.

Guilt and Perception: Some individuals feel guilty or view self-care as selfish, especially if they are accustomed to prioritizing others' needs over their own.

Lack of Awareness: Many people are unaware of what self-care entails or how to incorporate it into their lives effectively.

1. Establishing Healthy Boundaries

Setting boundaries involves defining limits in relationships and responsibilities to protect one's well-being and ensure a balance between personal and professional life.

Learn to Say No: Politely decline requests or commitments that overwhelm you or interfere with your self-care. This helps prevent burnout and preserves energy for essential activities.

Communicate Clearly: Express your needs and limits to others clearly and assertively. Effective communication ensures that boundaries are respected and understood.

Prioritize Your Needs: Make self-care a non-negotiable part of your routine. Schedule time for activities that recharge you, and protect this time from being encroached upon by other demands.

2. Practicing Physical Self-Care

Physical self-care involves taking actions to maintain your physical health and well-being. It is foundational to overall mental health.

Maintain a Balanced Diet: Eating nutritious foods that fuel your body can improve energy levels, mood, and cognitive function. Avoid excessive consumption of unhealthy foods that can contribute to physical and mental fatigue.

Exercise Regularly: Engage in physical activities that you enjoy, such as walking, yoga, or dancing. Regular exercise can reduce stress, enhance mood, and improve physical health.

Ensure Adequate Sleep: Prioritize sleep by establishing a regular sleep routine and creating a restful environment. Adequate sleep is crucial for mental clarity, emotional stability, and overall health.

3. Engaging in Emotional Self-Care

Emotional self-care involves actions that help you understand, process, and express your emotions healthily.

Express Your Feelings: Find outlets to express your emotions, such as talking to a friend, journaling, or engaging in creative activities like art or music.

Practice Self-Compassion: Treat yourself with kindness and understanding, especially during difficult times. Avoid self-criticism and focus on self-acceptance and forgiveness.

Seek Professional Support: If you are struggling with emotional challenges, consider seeking help from a mental health professional. Therapy can provide valuable tools and support for managing emotions and building emotional resilience.

4. Incorporating Mental Self-Care

Mental self-care focuses on activities that stimulate your mind and promote mental well-being.

Engage in Hobbies: Pursue activities that you find intellectually stimulating and enjoyable, such as reading, puzzles, or learning a new skill. Hobbies can provide a sense of accomplishment and relaxation.

Limit Information Overload: Be mindful of the information you consume, particularly from news and social media. Overexposure to negative or overwhelming information can increase stress and anxiety.

Practice Mindfulness: Incorporate mindfulness practices into your daily routine to enhance focus and mental clarity. Techniques such as meditation, deep breathing, and mindfulness exercises can help reduce stress and improve mental well-being.

5. Nurturing Spiritual Self-Care

Spiritual self-care involves connecting with your inner self and exploring activities that give your life meaning and purpose. It can encompass religious practices, personal reflection, or a connection to nature and the universe.

Explore Spiritual Practices: Engage in activities that align with your beliefs and values, such as prayer, meditation, or attending religious services. These practices can provide a sense of peace and connection.

Reflect on Personal Values: Take time to consider what is truly important to you and how you can align your actions with your core values. This can enhance your sense of purpose and fulfillment.

Connect with Nature: Spending time in nature can foster a sense of awe and tranquility. Activities like walking in the park, hiking, or gardening can help you feel more grounded and connected to the world around you.

6. Balancing Work and Life

Maintaining a balance between work and personal life is crucial for mental wellness. Work-life balance helps prevent burnout and ensures that you have time for self-care and personal activities.

Set Boundaries: Clearly delineate between work and personal time. Avoid bringing work-related tasks into personal time and create a physical or mental separation between work and home.

Prioritize Tasks: Identify and focus on the most important tasks to avoid feeling overwhelmed. Use time management techniques, such as setting specific goals and deadlines, to manage your workload effectively.

Take Breaks: Incorporate regular breaks into your workday to rest and recharge. Short breaks can improve productivity and reduce stress, preventing burnout.

7. Developing a Self-Care Plan

A self-care plan is a personalized approach to integrating self-care practices into your daily life. It involves identifying your needs, setting goals, and establishing routines that support your mental, emotional, and physical well-being.

Identify Your Needs: Assess different areas of your life to determine where you need more support or attention. Consider physical, emotional, mental, and spiritual needs when developing your plan.

Set Specific Goals: Establish clear, achievable goals for your self-care activities. For example, aim to exercise three times a week, practice mindfulness daily, or spend more time with loved ones.

Create a Routine: Incorporate self-care practices into your daily schedule. Establishing routines can help you consistently prioritize self-care and make it a regular part of your life.

Chapter 5
Mindfulness and
Meditation

Techniques for Reducing Stress and Anxiety

Mindfulness and meditation are powerful tools for managing stress and anxiety. They involve practices that cultivate awareness, presence, and relaxation, helping individuals respond to life's challenges with greater calm and clarity. This chapter explores various mindfulness and meditation techniques, their benefits, and how to integrate them into daily life for enhanced mental wellness.

Understanding Mindfulness and Meditation

Definition and Importance: Mindfulness is the practice of paying attention to the present moment with openness and without judgment. Meditation involves techniques to focus the mind and achieve a state of relaxation and awareness. Both practices are essential for reducing stress and anxiety, enhancing emotional regulation, and improving overall well-being.

Benefits of Mindfulness and Meditation: Research has shown that mindfulness and meditation offer numerous mental and physical health benefits, including:

Reduced Stress: Mindfulness helps individuals manage stress by promoting relaxation and reducing the physiological impact of stressors.

Improved Emotional Regulation: Regular practice can enhance the ability to manage and respond to emotions effectively, reducing the risk of anxiety and depression.

Enhanced Focus and Attention: Mindfulness and meditation improve cognitive function, including attention, concentration, and memory.

Better Physical Health: These practices can lower blood pressure, improve sleep, and boost the immune system.

Techniques for Practicing Mindfulness

1. Mindful Breathing

Mindful breathing involves focusing on the breath to anchor attention and promote relaxation. It is a simple yet effective technique for managing stress and anxiety.

Find a Comfortable Position: Sit or lie down in a comfortable position. Close your eyes and take a few deep breaths to relax your body.

Focus on Your Breath: Pay attention to the sensation of your breath as it enters and leaves your nostrils or the rise and fall of your chest or abdomen.

Observe Without Judgment: Notice any thoughts or distractions that arise and gently bring your focus back to your breath. Practice observing these thoughts without judgment or attachment.

2. Body Scan Meditation

Body scan meditation involves directing attention to different parts of the body to promote relaxation and awareness.

Lie Down Comfortably: Lie down in a comfortable position and close your eyes. Take a few deep breaths to relax.

Scan Your Body: Start from your toes and gradually move up to your head, focusing on each body part. Notice any sensations, tension, or discomfort.

Release Tension: As you focus on each body part, consciously relax and release any tension. Continue until you have scanned your entire body.

3. Mindful Eating

Mindful eating involves paying full attention to the experience of eating, including the taste, texture, and smell of food.

Choose a Meal or Snack: Select a meal or snack and sit down in a quiet, distraction-free environment.
Focus on the Experience: Take small bites and chew slowly, paying attention to the taste, texture, and sensation of the food. Notice the colors, smells, and appearance of your food.
Appreciate the Moment: Practice gratitude for the food and the experience of eating. Avoid multitasking or rushing through your meal.

4. Mindful Walking

Mindful walking involves paying attention to the experience of walking, including the movement of your body and your surroundings.
Find a Suitable Location: Choose a quiet, safe place for walking, such as a park or a quiet street.
Focus on Your Steps: Pay attention to the sensation of your feet touching the ground, the

movement of your legs, and the rhythm of your steps.

Observe Your Surroundings: Notice the sights, sounds, and smells around you as you walk. Stay present in the moment without focusing on your destination.

5. Mindfulness in Daily Activities

Incorporate mindfulness into everyday activities to enhance awareness and presence throughout your day.

Daily Tasks: Practice mindfulness while doing routine tasks, such as washing dishes, brushing your teeth, or folding laundry. Focus on the sensations and movements involved in the activity.

Mindful Listening: Pay full attention to conversations and listen without judgment or distraction. Focus on the speaker's words, tone, and body language.

Mindful Observing: Take moments throughout your day to pause and observe your surroundings. Notice details you might usually overlook and appreciate the present moment.

Techniques for Practicing Meditation

1. Guided Meditation

Guided meditation involves following instructions provided by a narrator or audio recording to achieve a meditative state.

Choose a Guided Meditation: Select a guided meditation that suits your needs, such as stress relief, relaxation, or focus. Many resources are available online or through meditation apps.
Find a Quiet Space: Sit or lie down in a comfortable position in a quiet environment. Close your eyes and listen to the guidance.
Follow the Instructions: Allow the narrator's voice to guide you through the meditation. Focus on the imagery, sensations, or themes described in the session.

2. Loving-Kindness Meditation
Loving-kindness meditation (Metta) involves cultivating feelings of compassion and kindness towards oneself and others.

Find a Comfortable Position: Sit or lie down in a comfortable position. Close your eyes and take a few deep breaths.

Generate Loving-Kindness: Begin by focusing on yourself and silently repeat phrases such as, "May I be happy, may I be healthy, may I be safe, may I be at peace."

Extend to Others: Gradually extend these wishes to others, starting with loved ones, then acquaintances, and finally all beings. Include individuals you may have conflicts with to foster compassion and forgiveness.

3. Transcendental Meditation

Transcendental meditation involves using a mantra or sound to achieve a deep state of relaxation and awareness.

Choose a Mantra: Select a word or phrase that resonates with you. Traditional mantras or sounds can also be used.

Find a Quiet Space: Sit comfortably with your eyes closed in a quiet environment.

Repeat the Mantra: Silently repeat the mantra in your mind. Focus on the sound and rhythm of the mantra, allowing it to guide you into a meditative state. Continue for about 20 minutes.

4. Visualization Meditation

Visualization meditation involves imagining a peaceful scene or situation to promote relaxation and mental clarity.

Choose a Peaceful Scene: Think of a place that makes you feel calm and relaxed, such as a beach, forest, or mountain.
Find a Quiet Space: Sit or lie down in a comfortable position. Close your eyes and take a few deep breaths.
Visualize the Scene: Imagine yourself in the chosen scene. Use all your senses to create a vivid mental image. Notice the sights, sounds, smells, and sensations of the environment.

5. Zen Meditation (Zazen)

Zen meditation, or Zazen, is a form of seated meditation that focuses on breath and posture to achieve mindfulness and inner peace.

Find a Quiet Space: Sit in a quiet place on a cushion or chair. Keep your back straight and your hands resting comfortably.

Focus on Your Breath: Pay attention to your breathing, observing each inhalation and exhalation. You can count your breaths to maintain focus.

Maintain Awareness: Allow thoughts to come and go without attachment. Gently bring your focus back to your breath if your mind wanders.

Integrating Mindfulness and Meditation into Daily Life

1. Create a Routine

Establishing a consistent routine for mindfulness and meditation helps make these practices a regular part of your life, enhancing their effectiveness over time.

Start Small: Begin with short sessions, such as 5-10 minutes, and gradually increase the duration as you become more comfortable with the practice. Consistency is more important than length.

Choose a Time: Find a time of day that works best for you, such as in the morning to set a positive tone for the day, or in the evening to unwind before bed. Stick to this time to build a habit.

Create a Space: Designate a specific space for mindfulness and meditation. This space should be quiet, comfortable, and free from distractions to foster relaxation and focus.

2. Use Technology and Resources

Leverage technology and available resources to support your mindfulness and meditation practice.

Meditation Apps: Use apps like Headspace, Calm, or Insight Timer, which offer guided meditations, mindfulness exercises, and tracking features to help you stay on track.
Online Resources: Explore online platforms that provide free guided meditations, instructional videos, and articles on mindfulness techniques. Many resources cater to different levels and needs.
Books and Courses: Consider reading books on mindfulness and meditation or enrolling in courses or workshops to deepen your understanding and practice.

3. Integrate Mindfulness into Daily Activities

Practice mindfulness throughout your day by integrating it into routine activities. This approach helps maintain a mindful mindset and reduces stress in various contexts.

Mindful Commuting: Use your commute as an opportunity for mindfulness. Pay attention to the sights and sounds around you, or practice mindful breathing to stay present.

Mindful Working: Apply mindfulness techniques at work, such as taking brief mindful breaks, focusing fully on one task at a time, and practicing deep breathing during stressful moments.

Mindful Interactions: Be present in your interactions with others. Listen actively, engage fully, and respond thoughtfully, enhancing the quality of your relationships.

4. Practice Mindfulness in Moments of Stress

Mindfulness can be particularly valuable in managing stress and anxiety. Use mindfulness techniques during challenging moments to maintain composure and perspective.

Pause and Breathe: When feeling overwhelmed, take a moment to pause and focus on your breath. Deep breathing can help calm your nervous system and provide clarity.

Grounding Techniques: Use grounding techniques, such as focusing on the physical sensations of your body or your surroundings, to stay anchored in the present moment during stressful situations.

Reflect and Respond: Before reacting to stress, take a moment to reflect on your emotions and thoughts. Respond mindfully rather than reacting impulsively, which can reduce anxiety and improve decision-making.

5. Combine Mindfulness and Meditation with Other Self-Care Practices

Integrate mindfulness and meditation with other self-care activities to create a holistic approach to mental wellness.

Exercise and Mindfulness: Combine physical exercise with mindfulness, such as practicing mindful walking, yoga, or tai chi. This integration enhances both physical and mental benefits.

Nutrition and Mindfulness: Practice mindful eating to develop a healthier relationship with food. Pay attention to hunger cues, savor each bite, and avoid distractions while eating.

Sleep and Meditation: Use meditation techniques to improve sleep quality. Guided sleep meditations or body scans can help relax your mind and prepare your body for restful sleep.

6. Track Your Progress and Reflect

Regularly track your mindfulness and meditation practice to monitor your progress and reflect on its impact on your mental wellness.

Keep a Journal: Maintain a journal to record your mindfulness and meditation experiences, noting any changes in your stress levels, mood, or overall well-being. Reflecting on your practice can provide insights and motivation.

Set Goals: Establish short-term and long-term goals for your mindfulness and meditation practice. Tracking progress towards these goals can help maintain focus and commitment.

Evaluate and Adjust: Periodically evaluate your practice to identify what works best for you and make necessary adjustments. Flexibility allows you to adapt your practice to changing needs and preferences.

Strategies for Mental Wellness

Building resilience, prioritizing self-care, and integrating mindfulness and meditation into daily life are essential strategies for maintaining mental wellness. These practices empower individuals to cope with stress, reduce anxiety, and enhance overall well-being.

Building Resilience: Resilience involves developing a growth mindset, strengthening emotional regulation, enhancing social support, fostering optimism, building self-efficacy, and cultivating adaptability. These skills enable individuals to navigate life's challenges with confidence and stability.

The Power of Self-Care: Self-care is crucial for maintaining mental health and preventing burnout. Effective self-care includes establishing healthy boundaries, practicing physical, emotional, and mental self-care, nurturing spiritual well-being, balancing work and life, and developing a personalized self-care plan.

Mindfulness and Meditation: Mindfulness and meditation offer powerful tools for reducing stress and anxiety. Techniques such as mindful breathing, body scan meditation, mindful eating, and various meditation practices help cultivate awareness, presence, and relaxation. Integrating these practices into daily routines and leveraging available resources enhances their benefits.

By adopting these strategies, individuals can foster a more resilient, balanced, and mindful approach to life, ultimately promoting mental wellness and a higher quality of life. Consistent practice and a commitment to self-care are key to reaping the long-term benefits of these mental wellness strategies.

Chapter 6

Social Media Strategies for Mental Wellness

Social media has become an integral part of modern life, shaping how we communicate, share information, and perceive the world. While it offers numerous benefits, such as connecting with others and accessing information, it also poses significant challenges to mental wellness. Excessive use, negative content, and online interactions can contribute to stress, anxiety, and a sense of inadequacy. Developing strategies for managing social media use is crucial for maintaining mental wellness. This section explores comprehensive approaches to setting boundaries, leveraging social media positively, and building supportive online communities.

Setting Boundaries: How to Manage Your Social Media Use

Setting boundaries around social media use is essential for protecting mental health. Boundaries help individuals avoid the pitfalls of excessive use, such as decreased productivity, heightened anxiety, and exposure to negative content. Effective boundary-setting involves awareness of social media's impact, self-regulation, and intentional use.

1. Conduct a Self-Audit

Evaluate your current social media habits to understand how, when, and why you use these platforms. This assessment helps identify areas for improvement and informs boundary-setting.

Track Usage: Use built-in tools or apps to monitor how much time you spend on social media each day. Pay attention to patterns, such as peak usage times and triggers for opening apps.

Identify Purpose: Reflect on the primary reasons for your social media use, such as connecting with friends, staying informed, or entertainment. Understanding your motivations helps set purposeful boundaries.

Notice Emotional Impact: Observe how social media affects your emotions. Do you feel anxious, stressed, or inadequate after using social media? Identifying these feelings can guide boundary-setting.

2. Set Clear Goals

Define specific goals for your social media use to ensure it aligns with your values and supports your well-being.

Purpose-Driven Use: Establish clear purposes for using social media, such as networking, learning, or staying connected. Avoid mindless scrolling by aligning usage with these goals.

Time Limits: Set daily or weekly limits for social media use. Use built-in tools to track and enforce these limits. For example, limit social media to one hour per day or designate specific times for checking apps.

Content Selection: Choose the type of content you want to engage with, such as positive, educational, or inspirational material. Avoid content that triggers negative emotions or anxiety.

Implementing Boundaries

1. Create a Schedule

Structure your social media use by creating a schedule that includes designated times for checking and engaging with social media. This approach helps prevent mindless scrolling and promotes intentional use.

Set Specific Times: Allocate specific times for social media use, such as during breaks or after work. Stick to these times to avoid constant checking and distraction.

Digital Detox Periods: Incorporate regular breaks from social media, such as a digital detox day each week. These breaks provide mental rest and reduce dependency on social media.

2. Use Technology to Enforce Boundaries

Leverage technology to help enforce social media boundaries. Various apps and features can assist in managing and controlling usage.

Screen Time Tools: Utilize screen time management tools available on smartphones to set app usage limits, schedule downtime, and receive usage reports.

App Blockers: Install app blockers or time management apps that restrict access to social media during certain hours or after a set usage limit is reached.

Notifications Management: Turn off non-essential notifications to reduce interruptions and the compulsion to check social media. Customize notification settings to receive only critical alerts.

3. **Curate Your Feed**

Mindfully curate your social media feed to ensure it aligns with your values and supports your well-being.

Follow Positive Accounts: Follow accounts that inspire, educate, or uplift you. Seek out content creators and communities that promote positivity and well-being.

Unfollow or Mute Negative Content: Unfollow or mute accounts that contribute to negative feelings, such as stress, envy, or frustration. Regularly review your feed and adjust accordingly.

Engage Mindfully: Be selective about the content you engage with. Avoid engaging in negative discussions or consuming content that does not contribute to your goals or well-being.

4. **Establish Physical Boundaries**

Set physical boundaries to create a clear separation between social media use and other activities.

Designate Social Media Zones: Limit social media use to specific areas, such as a desk or living room, and avoid using it in places like the bedroom or dining area to maintain boundaries between activities.

Device-Free Zones: Establish device-free zones in your home or work environment to encourage offline interactions and activities. For example, keep phones out of the bedroom to promote better sleep.

5. Practice Mindfulness

Incorporate mindfulness techniques to become more aware of your social media habits and their impact on your well-being.

Mindful Checking: Before opening a social media app, pause and ask yourself why you are doing it. Consider whether it aligns with your goals or is a reaction to boredom or stress.

Mindful Scrolling: As you scroll through your feed, pay attention to your emotions and thoughts. Notice how content affects you and make conscious choices about what to engage with or ignore.

Managing Social Media and Personal Relationships

1. Balance Online and Offline Interactions

Maintain a healthy balance between online interactions and in-person relationships to foster meaningful connections and reduce social isolation.

Prioritize Face-to-Face Interactions: Schedule regular face-to-face meetings with friends and family. Use social media to complement, not replace, real-life interactions.

Limit Social Media During Social Events: Avoid excessive social media use during social events. Focus on engaging with the people around you and being present in the moment.

2. Communicate Boundaries with Others

Communicate your social media boundaries to friends and family to foster understanding and support.

Explain Your Goals: Share your goals for managing social media use with close friends and family. Explain how these boundaries benefit your well-being and relationships.

Encourage Mutual Respect: Encourage mutual respect for boundaries in online interactions. Discuss acceptable times and methods for online communication to align expectations.

3. Reflect on Your Progress

Regularly reflect on your progress in managing social media use to ensure your boundaries are effective and supportive of your mental wellness.

Review Goals: Periodically review your social media goals and adjust as needed. Consider whether your boundaries are helping you achieve your objectives and maintain well-being.

Seek Feedback: Seek feedback from trusted friends or family members on how your social media habits impact your interactions and relationships. Use their insights to refine your boundaries.

Positive Social Media: How to Use Social Media for Good

Harnessing Social Media for Positive Outcomes

Social media can be a powerful tool for positive outcomes when used intentionally. It offers opportunities for personal growth, social connection, and contributing to the greater good. This chapter explores strategies for leveraging social media to enhance well-being, promote positivity, and make a meaningful impact.

Promoting Positive Content

1. Share Uplifting and Inspirational Content

Use social media to share content that inspires, motivates, and uplifts others. Positive content can create a ripple effect, fostering a supportive and encouraging online environment.

Personal Achievements: Share your personal achievements, milestones, and successes to inspire and motivate others. Celebrate your accomplishments and encourage others to share their wins.

Inspirational Quotes: Post quotes that resonate with you and promote positivity, resilience, and growth. Choose quotes that reflect your values and experiences.

Acts of Kindness: Highlight acts of kindness and positive initiatives, whether your own or those of others. Share stories that demonstrate the power of kindness and community.

2. Engage in Constructive Discussions

Participate in discussions that promote constructive dialogue, empathy, and understanding. Engaging positively in online conversations can contribute to a more respectful and inclusive digital space.

Respectful Communication: Communicate respectfully and thoughtfully in online discussions. Avoid engaging in arguments or negative exchanges. Focus on understanding different perspectives and contributing positively.

Supportive Comments: Leave supportive and encouraging comments on posts that resonate with you. Acknowledge the efforts and experiences of others, and provide constructive feedback when appropriate.

Promote Civil Discourse: Advocate for civil discourse and encourage others to engage in respectful conversations. Set an example by handling disagreements with grace and empathy.

3. Amplify Positive Messages and Causes

Use your social media platform to amplify positive messages and support causes that matter to you. Sharing content that aligns with your values can inspire others and contribute to meaningful change.

Support Social Causes: Share information about social causes, charities, or movements that you support. Use your platform to raise awareness and encourage others to get involved.

Promote Educational Content: Share educational resources, articles, or videos that provide valuable information and promote learning. Focus on content that contributes to personal growth and community well-being.

Highlight Positive Initiatives: Amplify positive initiatives, such as community projects, volunteer opportunities, or success stories. Use your voice to spotlight efforts that make a positive impact.

Building a Positive Online Presence

1. Develop a Personal Brand

Cultivate a personal brand that reflects your values, goals, and the positive impact you wish to make. A well-defined personal brand can help guide your social media activity and interactions.

Identify Your Values: Reflect on your core values and what you want to represent online. Consider how these values can guide your content and interactions.

Create Consistent Messaging: Develop consistent messaging and themes that align with your values. Use your bio, posts, and interactions to convey your personal brand clearly.

Engage Authentically: Engage authentically with your audience. Share your genuine thoughts, experiences, and perspectives, and avoid presenting a false or idealized version of yourself.

2. Use Social Media for Learning and Growth

Social media platforms offer valuable opportunities for learning, personal development, and skill enhancement. By curating your feed and engaging with educational content, you can leverage social media as a tool for continuous learning.

Follow Thought Leaders and Experts: Identify thought leaders, industry experts, and educators in your field of interest. Follow their profiles and engage with their content to gain insights, stay updated on trends, and expand your knowledge.

Join Communities and Groups: Participate in online communities, groups, or forums related to your hobbies, professional interests, or personal development goals. These spaces provide opportunities for learning, sharing experiences, and connecting with like-minded individuals.

Attend Webinars and Live Sessions: Many organizations and individuals host webinars, live sessions, and virtual events on social media platforms. Participate in these sessions to acquire new skills, receive expert guidance, and engage in interactive learning experiences.

Share Your Knowledge: Contribute to discussions and share your knowledge and expertise with others. By offering valuable insights, tips, or resources, you can establish yourself as a knowledgeable and supportive member of your online community.

3. Cultivate Positive Relationships

Social media can facilitate meaningful connections and supportive relationships when used intentionally. Building and nurturing positive relationships online contributes to emotional well-being and a sense of belonging.

Connect with Friends and Family: Use social media to stay connected with friends, family members, and loved ones, especially those who live far away. Share updates, photos, and messages to maintain strong relationships and celebrate milestones together.

Supportive Networks: Engage with online communities and networks that share your interests, values, or experiences. Participate in discussions, offer support to others, and seek advice or encouragement when needed.

Build Professional Connections: Network with professionals in your industry or field of expertise. Connect with colleagues, mentors, and potential collaborators to exchange ideas, explore career opportunities, and expand your professional network.

Reach Out for Support: Reach out to your online network for emotional support during challenging times. Share your experiences, seek advice, or simply connect with others who understand and can offer empathy and encouragement.

4. **Practice Digital Wellness**

Maintaining digital wellness is essential for balancing social media use with overall well-being. Adopting healthy habits and mindful practices promotes a positive relationship with technology and reduces potential negative impacts on mental health.

Set Intentional Use: Define clear intentions for your social media use and prioritize activities that align with your goals, values, and well-being. Avoid mindless scrolling or excessive screen time.

Take Breaks: Schedule regular breaks from social media to recharge, focus on offline activities, and reduce digital overwhelm. Disconnecting periodically can improve concentration, productivity, and overall mental clarity.

Establish Tech-Free Times: Designate specific times or days as tech-free zones to promote face-to-face interactions, engage in hobbies, or unwind without digital distractions.

Practice Mindful Consumption: Be mindful of the content you consume on social media. Evaluate its relevance, impact on your mood, and contribution to your well-being. Unfollow accounts or mute content that triggers negative emotions or distractions.

The Power of Community: Building Support Networks Through Social Media

Harnessing the Strength of Online Communities

Social media platforms serve as powerful catalysts for building and nurturing supportive communities. These digital spaces facilitate connections, foster collaboration, and provide valuable resources and emotional support. Building robust support networks through social media enhances mental wellness and promotes a sense of belonging.

Identifying and Joining Supportive Communities

1. Explore Interest-Based Communities

Discover and join online communities that align with your interests, passions, or personal goals. Whether you're interested in fitness, mental health, creative arts, or professional development, there are communities tailored to diverse interests and needs.

Search and Join Groups: Use platform-specific features to search for groups, forums, or pages related to your interests. Join communities that resonate with your values, provide valuable insights, and encourage meaningful interactions.

Evaluate Community Culture: Assess the culture and dynamics of potential communities before joining. Look for inclusive, supportive environments where members share knowledge, offer encouragement, and respect diverse perspectives.

Engage Actively: Participate actively in discussions, share relevant content, and contribute insights or experiences. Building rapport with community members fosters connections, promotes mutual support, and enriches your online experience.

2. Seek Professional and Peer Support

Social media platforms offer opportunities to connect with both professionals and peers who can offer expertise, guidance, and encouragement.

Connect with Experts: Follow professionals, thought leaders, or organizations in your field of interest or expertise. Engage with their content, attend virtual events or webinars, and seek advice or mentorship opportunities.

Peer Support Networks: Engage with peers who share similar experiences, challenges, or goals. Participate in peer support groups, online forums, or social media campaigns that promote solidarity, empathy, and shared learning.

Virtual Support Groups: Join virtual support groups dedicated to specific topics such as mental health, chronic illness, caregiving, or personal development. These groups offer a safe space for sharing experiences, accessing resources, and receiving emotional support.

Building Meaningful Connections

1. Foster Authentic Relationships

Nurture authentic relationships with community members based on trust, respect, and mutual support. Authentic connections enhance emotional well-being, foster a sense of belonging, and cultivate a supportive online environment.

Engage Thoughtfully: Listen actively, respond empathetically, and contribute constructively to discussions. Show genuine interest in others' experiences, perspectives, and contributions.

Offer Support: Extend support and encouragement to community members facing challenges or seeking guidance. Offer practical advice, share resources, or simply lend a listening ear.

Celebrate Successes: Celebrate milestones, achievements, and positive developments within the community. Acknowledge and applaud members' accomplishments to reinforce a culture of positivity and encouragement.

2. Contribute Positively to the Community

Contribute to the community's growth and well-being by sharing valuable insights, resources, and positive contributions.

Share Knowledge and Resources: Share informative articles, helpful tips, or relevant resources that benefit community members. Provide insights based on your expertise, experiences, or research to enrich discussions and enhance learning.

Create Inspiring Content: Create and share content that inspires, motivates, or educates community members. Use your platform to promote positivity, resilience, and personal growth.

Collaborate and Co-create: Collaborate with community members on projects, initiatives, or campaigns that align with shared goals or interests. Collective efforts promote collaboration, creativity, and community cohesion.

Supporting Mental Wellness Through Community Engagement

1. Seek Emotional Support

Reach out to community members for emotional support during challenging times, transitions, or personal struggles.

Share Vulnerabilities: Share your vulnerabilities, challenges, or concerns within the community. Expressing emotions and seeking support can alleviate feelings of isolation and promote emotional resilience.
Receive Validation: Receive validation, empathy, and encouragement from community members who understand your experiences and offer compassionate support.
Access Peer Perspectives: Gain diverse perspectives, insights, and coping strategies from peers who have faced similar challenges. Peer

support fosters mutual learning, emotional connection, and personal growth.

2. **Provide Peer Support**

Offer empathetic support, encouragement, and practical advice to community members navigating difficulties or seeking guidance.

Empower Others: Empower individuals by offering empowering messages, affirmations, or motivational resources. Encourage self-compassion, resilience, and proactive coping strategies.

Share Personal Experiences: Share your experiences, lessons learned, or coping strategies that may resonate with and benefit others. Personal stories inspire hope, provide reassurance, and promote solidarity within the community.

Refer to Resources: Refer community members to relevant resources, support services, or professional guidance when appropriate. Connect individuals with resources that address their specific needs and promote holistic well-being.

3. **Foster a Sense of Belonging**

Cultivate a sense of belonging, inclusion, and community spirit among members to enhance emotional well-being and collective support.

Create Welcoming Spaces: Create welcoming, inclusive spaces where members feel valued, respected, and accepted. Foster a culture of openness, diversity, and mutual respect within the community.

Encourage Engagement: Encourage active participation, collaboration, and contribution from all members. Facilitate discussions, activities, or initiatives that promote community engagement and connection.

Celebrate Diversity: Celebrate the diversity of experiences, backgrounds, and perspectives within the community. Embrace differences as strengths that enrich collective learning, understanding, and community cohesion.

Navigating Challenges and Resolving Conflicts

1. Address Challenges Constructively

Navigate challenges, conflicts, or disagreements within the community with respect, empathy, and a commitment to mutual understanding.

Practice Active Listening: Listen attentively to different viewpoints, concerns, or grievances expressed by community members. Demonstrate empathy, validate emotions, and seek clarity to understand underlying issues.

Seek Common Ground: Identify common goals, values, or interests shared by community members to foster common ground and facilitate constructive dialogue. Focus on areas of agreement and collaboration to build consensus and resolve conflicts.

Encourage Mediation: Facilitate mediation or conflict resolution processes to address disputes or tensions within the community. Seek neutral facilitators or mediators who can promote communication, clarify misunderstandings, and guide the resolution process.

2. Promote Positive Communication Norms

Establish positive communication norms, guidelines, or codes of conduct to promote respectful, inclusive, and constructive interactions within the community.

Set Clear Expectations: Define clear expectations regarding respectful communication, constructive feedback, and conflict resolution within the community. Communicate guidelines, rules, or codes of conduct that align with shared values and promote a supportive environment.

Model Positive Behavior: Lead by example and model positive communication, empathy,and respect in all interactions. Demonstrate how to engage in constructive dialogue, provide constructive feedback, and handle disagreements gracefully.

Encourage Accountability: Encourage accountability among community members to uphold communication norms and guidelines. Foster a culture where individuals feel empowered to speak up against harmful behavior and support positive interactions.

Provide Resources: Offer resources, workshops, or training on effective communication, conflict resolution, and emotional intelligence. Equip community members with skills and knowledge to navigate interactions positively.

Social media strategies for mental wellness involve setting effective boundaries, using social media positively, and leveraging the power of online communities for support and connection. By mindfully managing social media use, promoting positivity, and building inclusive, supportive networks, individuals can harness the benefits of social media while mitigating its potential negative impacts. This comprehensive approach enhances mental well-being, fosters meaningful connections, and empowers individuals to use social media as a tool for personal growth and community enrichment. Through intentional practices and community engagement, social media can become a platform that supports mental wellness and fosters a sense of belonging and empowerment in the digital age.

Chapter 7
Action Plan

A 30-Day Plan for Improving Mental Wellness and Managing Social Media

Developing an effective action plan is crucial for integrating strategies for mental wellness and managing social media use into daily life. This 30-day plan offers a structured approach, combining practical steps with a focus on creating lasting habits that promote mental health and a balanced digital lifestyle.

Week 1: Establishing the Foundation

Day 1: Self-Assessment and Goal Setting

1. Conduct a Self-Assessment

Journal Reflection: Reflect on your current mental wellness and social media habits. Identify areas of concern, such as stress triggers, social media addiction, or emotional challenges.

Set Baseline Metrics: Document how much time you spend on social media, your emotional state before and after usage, and any specific negative impacts on your mental health.

2. Set Clear Goals

Define Objectives: Set specific, measurable, achievable, relevant, and time-bound (SMART) goals related to mental wellness and social media use. Examples include reducing social media time by 30 minutes daily or practicing mindfulness exercises thrice a week.

Prioritize Goals: Rank your goals by importance and feasibility. Focus on a few key areas to avoid feeling overwhelmed.

Day 2: Create a Daily Routine

1. Design a Balanced Routine

Morning Ritual: Establish a morning routine that includes activities promoting mental clarity and well-being, such as journaling, stretching, or meditation.

Work/Study Blocks: Allocate dedicated time blocks for work or study without social media distractions. Use productivity techniques like the Pomodoro method to enhance focus.

Evening Wind-Down: Develop an evening routine that helps you unwind, such as reading, taking a bath, or practicing deep breathing exercises.

2. Schedule Breaks

Digital Breaks: Incorporate regular breaks throughout the day to step away from screens. Use this time for physical activity, relaxation, or connecting with loved ones.

Social Media Check-ins: Set specific times for checking social media, ensuring it doesn't interfere with essential tasks or relaxation time.

Day 3: Declutter Your Digital Space

1. Organize Social Media Accounts

Review Follows: Assess the accounts you follow and unfollow those that don't contribute positively to your well-being or align with your goals.
Clean Up Notifications: Turn off unnecessary notifications to reduce distractions and stress from constant alerts.

2. Curate Positive Content

Positive Feeds: Follow accounts that inspire, educate, or bring joy. Engage with content that uplifts and motivates you, such as educational channels, wellness influencers, or hobby-related pages.

Content Review: Regularly review and update your social media feeds to ensure they remain positive and aligned with your current interests.

Day 4: Practice Mindfulness

1. Introduce Mindfulness Practices

Daily Meditation: Start with short, guided meditations (5-10 minutes) focusing on breath awareness or body scans to cultivate mindfulness.
Mindful Breaks: Practice mindfulness during daily activities, such as eating or walking, by paying attention to your senses and surroundings.

2. Incorporate Mindful Social Media Use

Pause and Reflect: Before opening social media, pause and ask yourself why you're doing so. Reflect on whether it aligns with your goals or is a response to boredom or stress.
Mindful Browsing: Engage with content consciously, focusing on quality rather than quantity. Avoid mindless scrolling by setting time limits or using apps that track usage.

Day 5: Build a Support System

1. Identify Support Networks

Connect with Supportive People: Reach out to friends, family, or online communities that provide positive support and encouragement. Join groups or forums aligned with your interests or mental wellness goals.

Professional Support: Consider seeking guidance from a mental health professional or counselor if needed. Explore teletherapy options for convenient access.

2. Share Your Journey

Accountability Partners: Find an accountability partner to share your goals and progress with. Regular check-ins can provide motivation and support.

Community Engagement: Engage in discussions, share your experiences, and seek advice from online support groups or wellness communities.

Day 6: Focus on Physical Health

1. Integrate Physical Activity

Exercise Routine: Incorporate regular physical activity into your routine, such as walking, yoga, or home workouts. Aim for at least 30 minutes of moderate exercise most days.
Active Breaks: Use digital breaks for short bursts of physical activity, like stretching or a quick walk, to refresh your mind and body.

2. Prioritize Nutrition and Sleep

Healthy Eating: Focus on balanced meals rich in nutrients to support mental and physical health. Avoid excessive caffeine or sugar intake, which can impact mood and energy levels.
Sleep Hygiene: Establish a sleep schedule and create a relaxing bedtime routine. Limit screen time before bed to improve sleep quality.

Day 7: Reflect and Adjust

1. Weekly Reflection

Review Progress: Reflect on the past week's activities and achievements. Identify what worked well and what challenges you faced.
Adjust Goals: Modify your goals or strategies based on your experiences. Make necessary adjustments to improve your routine and mental wellness plan.

2. Celebrate Small Wins

Acknowledge Successes: Celebrate your progress and accomplishments, no matter how small. Positive reinforcement builds motivation and confidence.
Reward Yourself: Treat yourself to something enjoyable, like a favorite activity or a small indulgence, as a reward for your efforts.

Day 8: Develop Coping Strategies

1. Identify Stressors

Stress Inventory: Make a list of common stressors in your life, including work, relationships, or social media interactions.
Emotional Triggers: Identify specific triggers that impact your emotions negatively and consider their sources.

2. Create Coping Plans

Healthy Coping Mechanisms: Develop strategies for managing stress, such as deep breathing exercises, journaling, or talking to a friend.
Digital Detox: Plan regular digital detox periods, where you disconnect from social media and focus on offline activities to reduce stress and anxiety.

Day 9: Explore Self-Care Activities

1. Prioritize Self-Care

Daily Self-Care: Schedule daily self-care activities that bring joy and relaxation, such as reading, listening to music, or engaging in hobbies.
Weekly Self-Care: Plan more extended self-care sessions weekly, like spa treatments, nature walks, or creative projects.

2. Create a Self-Care Toolkit

Personalized Toolkit: Assemble a self-care toolkit with items and activities that soothe and comfort you, like favorite books, essential oils, or meditation apps.
Emergency Self-Care: Develop a list of quick self-care activities to use during high-stress moments, such as taking a few deep breaths, stretching, or stepping outside for fresh air.

Day 10: Build Resilience

1. Practice Resilience-Building Techniques

Positive Affirmations: Use positive affirmations to counter negative thoughts and build a resilient mindset. Repeat affirmations daily to reinforce self-belief.

Gratitude Practice: Keep a gratitude journal, noting things you're thankful for each day. Focusing on positives helps build emotional resilience.

2. Learn from Challenges

Reflect on Experiences: Reflect on past challenges and how you overcame them. Identify strengths and lessons learned that can be applied to future difficulties.

Growth Mindset: Adopt a growth mindset, viewing challenges as opportunities for learning and growth rather than setbacks.

Day 11: Strengthen Social Connections

1. Engage with Your Community

Online Engagement: Participate in online community discussions, share your experiences, and support others. Engaging with positive, like-minded individuals fosters a sense of belonging.

Offline Connections: Arrange to meet friends or family in person, or connect through phone calls or video chats. Strengthen offline relationships to balance digital interactions.

2. Plan Social Activities

Group Activities: Plan group activities or virtual meetups around shared interests, such as book clubs, hobby groups, or workout sessions.
Volunteer Opportunities: Explore volunteer opportunities in your community or through online platforms. Helping others enhances social connections and provides a sense of purpose.

Day 12: Manage Emotional Well-Being

1. Emotional Regulation Techniques

Emotional Awareness: Practice being aware of your emotions and understanding their origins. Use tools like mood trackers to identify patterns and triggers.
Emotional Expression: Find healthy ways to express your emotions, such as talking to a trusted friend, writing in a journal, or engaging in creative activities like drawing or music.

2. Build Emotional Resilience

Stress Management: Practice stress management techniques, such as progressive muscle relaxation, mindfulness, or guided imagery, to build emotional resilience.

Support Networks: Lean on your support networks during emotional challenges. Share your feelings and seek advice or comfort from those who understand.

Day 13: Foster Creativity

1. Explore Creative Outlets

Creative Hobbies: Engage in creative hobbies like painting, writing, cooking, or crafting. Creativity boosts mental wellness and provides a productive escape from stress.

Creative Expression: Use creative expression as a tool for processing emotions and exploring new perspectives. Try activities like journaling, photography, or dance.

2. Share Your Creativity

Social Sharing: Share your creative projects on social media or within your communities. Celebrating creativity with others fosters connection and inspiration.
Collaborative Projects: Collaborate on creative projects with friends or community members. Group creativity enhances teamwork and generates new ideas.

Day 14: Integrate Nature into Your Routine

1. Embrace Outdoor Activities

Daily Nature Walks: Incorporate daily walks in natural settings, such as parks, forests, or beaches, into your routine. Exposure to nature enhances mental clarity, reduces stress, and boosts mood.
Outdoor Exercise: Engage in outdoor physical activities, such as hiking, biking, or gardening, to benefit from both exercise and nature.

2. Create a Nature Connection

Indoor Plants: Introduce indoor plants into your living space to bring a touch of nature indoors.

Caring for plants can provide a sense of calm and satisfaction.

Nature Breaks: Take short breaks to step outside and connect with nature during your day. Even a few minutes of fresh air and sunlight can improve your mental well-being.

Week 3: Managing Social Media and Enhancing Mental Wellness

Day 15: Evaluate Social Media Usage

1. Review Social Media Habits

Usage Analysis: Use tools or apps to analyze your social media usage patterns. Identify which platforms you spend the most time on and what activities dominate your usage.

Emotional Impact: Reflect on the emotional impact of your social media interactions. Note any feelings of anxiety, comparison, or stress linked to specific activities or platforms.

2. Adjust Social Media Habits

Set Time Limits: Implement time limits for social media usage using built-in app features or third-party tools. Aim to reduce non-productive scrolling and prioritize meaningful interactions.

Curate Content: Continually curate your social media feeds to include positive, educational, and inspiring content. Unfollow accounts that contribute to negative emotions or stress.

Day 16: Foster Positive Social Media Engagement

1. Engage Positively

Constructive Comments: Focus on leaving constructive comments and positive feedback on posts. Support and uplift others through encouraging words and respectful dialogue.

Share Positivity: Share content that promotes positivity, such as inspirational quotes, success stories, or helpful resources. Become a source of encouragement within your social media circles.

2. Limit Negative Interactions

Avoid Conflicts: Steer clear of online conflicts, debates, or discussions that are likely to lead to negativity or stress. If a conversation becomes heated, disengage politely.

Block or Report: Utilize platform features to block or report users who engage in harassment, trolling, or abusive behavior. Protect your digital space from negativity.

Day 17: Develop a Digital Detox Routine

1. Plan Regular Digital Detoxes

Digital-Free Days: Schedule regular digital detox days where you completely disconnect from social media and digital devices. Use this time for offline activities and self-care.

Partial Detoxes: Implement partial digital detox periods each day, such as device-free mornings or evenings, to reduce screen time and improve mental clarity.

2. Create Offline Alternatives

Engaging Hobbies: Develop hobbies or interests that don't involve screens, such as reading, puzzles, or outdoor sports. These activities provide fulfilling alternatives to digital engagement.

Social Connections: Strengthen offline social connections by planning in-person meetups, phone calls, or video chats with friends and family.

Day 18: Cultivate Mindfulness in Social Media Use

1. Practice Mindful Browsing

Intentional Use: Approach social media use with intention. Before logging in, set a purpose for your activity, such as connecting with a friend, finding information, or sharing an update.

Reflect and Adjust: After using social media, take a moment to reflect on how it made you feel and whether it served your intended purpose. Adjust your usage patterns based on these reflections.

2. Apply Mindfulness Techniques

Breathing Exercises: Incorporate short breathing exercises or mindfulness practices before and after social media sessions to stay grounded and present.

Focused Interaction: Limit multitasking while on social media. Focus on one activity at a time, such as reading posts or responding to messages, to enhance mindful engagement.

Day 19: Enhance Online Privacy and Security

1. Review Privacy Settings

Privacy Controls: Regularly review and update your privacy settings on social media platforms to control who can see your content and how your data is used.

Profile Visibility: Adjust profile visibility settings to ensure that only trusted individuals or connections can view personal information.

2. Practice Safe Online Behavior

Strong Passwords: Use strong, unique passwords for social media accounts and change them regularly. Enable two-factor authentication for added security.

Be Cautious: Be cautious about sharing personal information online. Avoid posting sensitive details or engaging in interactions that could compromise your privacy or security.

Day 20: Utilize Technology for Well-Being

1. Explore Wellness Apps

Mental Health Apps: Use mental health apps that offer guided meditations, mood tracking, or stress management tools. These apps can support your mental wellness journey.
Productivity Tools: Implement productivity apps that help manage time, set goals, and track progress. Use these tools to maintain focus and balance social media use with other activities.

2. Set Up Digital Wellness Features

Screen Time Monitoring: Activate screen time monitoring features on your devices to track and manage usage. Set daily limits or use downtime settings to control access to apps.
Focus Modes: Utilize focus modes or do-not-disturb settings to minimize distractions during work, study, or relaxation periods.

Day 21: Review and Reflect

1. Weekly Check-In

Assess Progress: Reflect on your achievements and challenges over the past week. Assess your adherence to the action plan and identify areas for improvement.
Adjust Strategies: Make adjustments to your strategies and goals based on your experiences. Refine your approach to better align with your needs and objectives.

2. Celebrate Milestones

Acknowledge Achievements: Recognize and celebrate your progress and milestones. Small victories contribute to long-term success and motivation.
Reward Efforts: Treat yourself to something enjoyable as a reward for your hard work, such as a favorite activity or a relaxing treat.

Week 4: Long-Term Strategies for Sustaining Mental Wellness and Healthy Social Media Use

Day 22: Integrate Long-Term Mental Wellness Practices

1. Establish Ongoing Self-Care Routines

Routine Maintenance: Continue incorporating daily self-care activities that support your mental well-being, such as exercise, mindfulness, and creative pursuits.

Seasonal Adjustments: Adapt your self-care routines to accommodate changes in seasons, life circumstances, or evolving interests.

2. Develop a Resilience Plan

Resilience Strategies: Maintain and expand on resilience-building practices, such as positive affirmations, gratitude journaling, and learning from challenges.

Crisis Response: Create a crisis response plan outlining steps to take during high-stress or emotional periods, including support contacts, coping techniques, and emergency resources.

Day 23: Strengthen Social Media Boundaries

1. Reinforce Boundaries

Routine Boundaries: Maintain established boundaries around social media use, such as set times for engagement and digital detox periods.
Content Boundaries: Continue curating your social media feeds to align with your mental wellness goals, avoiding content that triggers stress or negative emotions.

2. Educate and Empower

Awareness: Stay informed about the latest trends and potential pitfalls in social media usage. Share your knowledge and experiences with others to promote healthy digital habits.
Empowerment: Encourage others to set their own social media boundaries and support them in adopting mindful practices.

Day 24: Cultivate Digital Well-Being

1. Practice Ongoing Digital Detox

Regular Detoxes: Incorporate regular digital detox periods into your schedule, such as device-free weekends or designated offline hours.

Technology-Free Zones: Create technology-free zones in your home, such as the bedroom or dining area, to foster a healthier relationship with digital devices.

2. Promote Digital Wellness

Wellness Advocacy: Advocate for digital wellness within your communities or workplaces by sharing resources, hosting workshops, or leading discussions on healthy digital habits.

Positive Influence: Use your social media presence to promote positive digital wellness practices and inspire others to adopt similar strategies.

Day 25: Enhance Online Engagement

1. Engage with Purpose

Intentional Interaction: Engage with social media purposefully, focusing on meaningful connections, informative content, and constructive discussions.

Community Contribution: Actively contribute to your online communities by sharing valuable insights, supporting others, and participating in collaborative projects.

2. Support Positive Movements

Social Causes: Use your platform to support positive social causes, advocacy efforts, or community initiatives. Amplify voices and movements that align with your values.

Awareness Campaigns: Participate in or create awareness campaigns that address mental wellness, digital well-being, or other important issues. Use your influence to spread positivity and knowledge.

Day 26: Foster Ongoing Learning and Growth

1. Continue Personal Development

Skill Development: Pursue personal development opportunities that enhance your skills, knowledge, and interests. Enroll in online courses, attend workshops, or engage in self-study.

Hobbies and Interests: Explore new hobbies or deepen existing interests. Continuous learning and engagement in fulfilling activities contribute to mental wellness and personal growth.

2. Stay Updated

Trends and Tools: Keep up with the latest trends, tools, and research related to mental wellness and social media. Apply new insights to refine your practices and strategies.

Peer Learning: Participate in peer learning opportunities, such as discussion groups, online forums, or collaborative projects, to exchange ideas and experiences.

Day 27: Monitor Mental Wellness Progress

1. Regular Assessments

Monthly Check-Ins: Conduct monthly self-assessments to review your mental wellness and social media habits. Reflect on any changes in mood, stress levels, and overall well-being since implementing your action plan.

Goal Review: Revisit your initial goals and evaluate your progress. Adjust your objectives as needed to ensure they remain relevant and achievable.

2. Use Tracking Tools

Mood Tracking: Utilize mood tracking apps or journals to record daily emotions and identify patterns over time. This helps in recognizing triggers and areas for improvement.

Usage Reports: Review social media usage reports from apps or devices to monitor your time spent online and identify areas where you can reduce or optimize use.

Day 28: Plan for Sustainable Changes

1. Develop Long-Term Habits

Habit Formation: Focus on turning positive behaviors into long-term habits. Use techniques such as habit stacking (linking new habits to established ones) or setting reminders to reinforce new routines.

Consistency: Strive for consistency in your mental wellness practices and social media management. Regularly engage in activities that promote well-being and balance.

2. Plan for Life Changes

Adapting Strategies: Prepare to adapt your mental wellness and social media strategies to life changes, such as new jobs, relocations, or changes in personal circumstances. Flexibility helps maintain progress despite shifts in your environment.

Support Systems: Strengthen your support systems by building relationships with individuals who can provide encouragement and accountability during transitions.

Day 29: Cultivate Positive Mindsets

1. Embrace Growth

Positive Mindset: Cultivate a positive mindset by focusing on growth and learning. View challenges as opportunities to develop resilience and gain new insights.

Affirmations: Continue using positive affirmations to reinforce self-confidence and a positive outlook. Create a list of affirmations that resonate with you and recite them daily.

2. Gratitude Practice

Daily Gratitude: Maintain a daily gratitude practice to enhance positivity. Write down at least three things you're grateful for each day, and reflect on the positive aspects of your life.

Gratitude Sharing: Share your gratitude with others, whether through thank-you notes, compliments, or expressions of appreciation. This fosters positive connections and uplifts both you and others.

Day 30: Celebrate and Reflect

1. Celebrate Achievements

Reflect on Successes: Take time to celebrate your achievements over the past month. Acknowledge the progress you've made in improving mental wellness and managing social media use.

Reward Yourself: Plan a special reward or treat for completing the 30-day plan. This reinforces positive behavior and provides motivation to continue your efforts.

2. Plan for the Future

Set New Goals: Based on your reflections and progress, set new goals for the coming months. Continue building on your successes and address any remaining challenges.

Sustained Effort: Commit to maintaining and refining the strategies you've developed. Regularly revisit and update your action plan to stay aligned with your evolving needs and circumstances.

Overcoming Obstacles: Common Challenges and How to Overcome Them

While implementing a plan for mental wellness and managing social media use, you may encounter various challenges. Recognizing these obstacles and developing strategies to overcome them is essential for sustained success.

Common Challenges

1. Inconsistent Motivation

Issue: Maintaining motivation can be difficult, especially when progress feels slow or setbacks occur.
Solution: Set small, achievable milestones to provide regular wins and boost motivation. Incorporate regular reflections to remind yourself of the benefits and progress made.

2. Social Pressure

Issue: Social pressure to stay constantly connected or participate in online activities can make it hard to manage social media use.

Solution: Communicate your boundaries clearly to friends and family. Find supportive communities that respect your goals and share your values regarding digital well-being.

3. Emotional Triggers

Issue: Negative emotions, such as anxiety or stress, can be exacerbated by social media interactions or content.
Solution: Identify and minimize exposure to emotional triggers by curating your social media feeds and using tools like muting or blocking. Practice emotional regulation techniques to manage reactions.

4. Time Management

Issue: Balancing social media use with other responsibilities can be challenging, leading to time management issues.
Solution: Use productivity tools and techniques, such as time blocking or setting specific social media schedules, to ensure balanced and productive use.

5. Lack of Support

Issue: A lack of support from peers or family can hinder your efforts to improve mental wellness and manage social media use.
Solution: Seek out like-minded individuals or groups who share your goals. Engage with online or offline communities that provide encouragement and accountability.

Overcoming Challenges

1. Develop Resilience

Build Resilience: Continuously practice resilience-building techniques, such as mindfulness, positive affirmations, and gratitude. Resilience helps you bounce back from setbacks and stay focused on your goals.
Learn from Setbacks: View challenges as learning opportunities rather than failures. Reflect on setbacks, identify lessons learned, and adjust your strategies accordingly.

2. Foster a Growth Mindset

Adopt Growth Perspective: Embrace a growth mindset by viewing personal development as an ongoing process. Recognize that improvement takes time and persistence, and celebrate incremental progress.

Stay Curious: Maintain a curiosity-driven approach to personal development. Explore new strategies, techniques, and tools to enhance your mental wellness and digital habits.

3. Utilize Support Networks

Seek Support: Regularly engage with your support networks, whether through online communities, friends, family, or professional counselors. Share your challenges and seek advice or encouragement when needed.

Provide Support: Actively support others who are on similar journeys. Sharing experiences and offering assistance creates a reciprocal support system that benefits everyone involved.

4. Prioritize Self-Care

Commit to Self-Care: Consistently prioritize self-care activities that nourish your mental and emotional well-being. Regular self-care helps maintain balance and resilience in the face of challenges.

Adapt Self-Care: Be flexible with your self-care routines, adapting them to your current needs and circumstances. Adjust your activities based on what feels most supportive at any given time.

5. Stay Informed

Continuous Learning: Keep learning about mental wellness, digital well-being, and effective social media management. Stay updated with new research, tools, and techniques to refine your strategies.
Resource Utilization: Utilize available resources, such as books, articles, podcasts, or workshops, to gain insights and inspiration for overcoming challenges and sustaining progress.

Chapter 8
Maintaining Progress

Long-Term Strategies for Sustaining Mental Wellness and Healthy Social Media Use

Sustaining mental wellness and healthy social media use requires ongoing commitment and adaptation. Developing long-term strategies helps ensure continued progress and resilience.

Sustaining Mental Wellness

1. Regularly Update Goals

Goal Review: Periodically review and update your mental wellness goals to reflect changes in your life and personal development. Set new objectives as you achieve previous ones.
Flexible Goals: Allow flexibility in your goals to accommodate evolving circumstances and needs. Adapt your strategies to stay relevant and effective.

2. Practice Lifelong Learning

Personal Development: Engage in lifelong learning activities that enhance your skills, knowledge, and well-being. Explore new interests, take courses, or participate in workshops to support continuous growth.

Wellness Education: Stay informed about the latest trends and research in mental wellness. Apply new insights to refine your practices and strategies.

3. Integrate Wellness into Daily Life

Daily Routines: Embed wellness practices into your daily routines, making them integral parts of your lifestyle. Activities like mindfulness, exercise, and creative hobbies should become habitual.

Seasonal Adjustments: Adapt your wellness routines to seasonal changes or shifts in your life, ensuring they remain supportive and relevant throughout the year.

4. Foster Positive Relationships

Strong Connections: Maintain and strengthen relationships that contribute positively to your well-being. Regularly connect with supportive friends, family, and communities.

Network Building: Expand your network by joining new communities or groups that align with your interests and values. Building a diverse support system enhances resilience and connection.

Sustaining Healthy Social Media Use

1. Establish Sustainable Boundaries

Ongoing Boundaries: Maintain established boundaries around social media use, such as designated usage times and digital detox periods. Regularly reassess and adjust these boundaries as needed.
Healthy Engagement: Focus on engaging with social media in ways that align with your well-being goals. Prioritize meaningful interactions and avoid activities that contribute to stress or negativity.

2. Promote Positive Digital Behavior
Mindful Use: Continue practicing mindful social media use, approaching interactions with intention and awareness. Reflect on your digital habits and make adjustments to enhance your experience.
Positive Influence: Use your social media presence to promote positive behavior, share valuable content, and support online communities. Be a role model for healthy digital engagement.

3. Adapt to Technological Changes

Technology Trends: Stay informed about technological advancements and trends that may impact social media use. Adapt your strategies to incorporate new tools or features that support well-being.

Digital Literacy: Enhance your digital literacy by learning about data privacy, security, and ethical online behavior. Protect yourself and others by practicing responsible digital citizenship.

4. Balance Digital and Offline Life

Offline Prioritization: Maintain a balance between digital activities and offline experiences. Prioritize offline hobbies, face-to-face interactions, and activities that provide enrichment and relaxation away from screens.

Digital Sabbaths: Schedule regular "digital sabbaths" where you take a break from all online activities. Use this time to engage in reflective, creative, or social activities that don't involve technology.

Foster Continuous Reflection and Adaptation

1. Regular Self-Reflection

Routine Check-Ins: Incorporate regular self-reflection into your routine, assessing your mental wellness and social media habits. Use journaling, meditation, or discussions with trusted friends to reflect on your experiences and identify areas for improvement.
Feedback Loops: Create feedback loops by regularly asking for feedback from friends or using self-assessment tools to understand how your habits impact your well-being. This can help you make informed adjustments to your strategies.

2. Embrace Change and Adaptation

Adaptability: Be open to change and ready to adapt your strategies as your life circumstances evolve. Whether it's a new job, a move, or a significant life event, flexibility is key to maintaining your progress.
Learning and Growth: View challenges and setbacks as opportunities for learning and growth. Adapt your approach based on what you learn from your experiences and the feedback you receive.

Build a Supportive Environment

1. Develop a Support Network

Community Engagement: Join or maintain connections with supportive communities, both online and offline, that align with your mental wellness and social media goals. Communities can provide encouragement, share insights, and offer accountability.
Professional Support: Don't hesitate to seek professional support when needed. Therapists, counselors, and coaches can offer valuable guidance and strategies for sustaining mental wellness and managing social media effectively.

2. Foster Positive Relationships

Nurture Connections: Focus on nurturing positive relationships that contribute to your well-being. Regularly invest time in activities and interactions that strengthen your bonds with family, friends, and colleagues.
Set Boundaries: Establish and maintain healthy boundaries in all relationships, including those with digital connections. Ensure that your interactions

are supportive and respectful of your mental wellness needs.

Cultivate Mindful Digital Consumption

1. Practice Digital Minimalism

Selective Engagement: Adopt a digital minimalism approach by carefully selecting the digital tools, apps, and platforms you use. Focus on those that add value to your life and eliminate or minimize use of those that don't.
Purpose-Driven Use: Before engaging with social media or other digital content, ask yourself what you hope to gain from the experience. Let this purpose guide your interactions and limit aimless browsing or scrolling.

2. Curate Content

Positive Feeds: Regularly curate your social media feeds and digital content to include sources of positivity, inspiration, and learning. Unfollow, mute, or block content that doesn't contribute to your well-being or aligns with your values.
Mindful Interaction: Interact with content and people on social media in ways that promote positivity and constructive engagement. Avoid

reactive behaviors and instead focus on thoughtful and intentional responses.

Integrate Wellness and Technology

1. Use Technology to Support Wellness

Wellness Apps: Leverage technology to support your mental wellness through apps and tools designed for meditation, stress management, mood tracking, and productivity. Choose apps that fit your specific needs and preferences.
Digital Wellness Tools: Utilize digital wellness tools that help you manage screen time, block distracting apps, and set reminders for breaks or wellness activities.

2. Explore New Technologies

Innovative Solutions: Stay open to exploring new technologies that can enhance your mental wellness and digital habits. This might include wearable devices, virtual reality wellness programs, or new mental health apps.
Ethical Tech Use: Adopt ethical tech use practices, being mindful of data privacy and the impact of technology on your well-being. Make informed

choices about how you share personal information and use digital services.

Commit to Lifelong Learning and Development

1. Continuous Education

Skill Building: Engage in continuous education and skill-building activities related to mental wellness and digital literacy. Attend workshops, take online courses, or read books on these topics to stay informed and competent.
Trends Awareness: Stay aware of trends in mental health and digital technology. Understanding emerging research and developments can help you refine your strategies and maintain effective practices.

2. Reflective Practice

Evaluate and Adjust: Regularly evaluate your practices and strategies, making adjustments as needed to ensure they remain effective and aligned with your goals. Use self-reflection and feedback to guide your adjustments.
Innovative Approaches: Be willing to try new approaches and techniques to support your mental

wellness and manage social media. Experiment with different methods and assess their impact on your well-being.

Foster a Balanced Lifestyle

1. Holistic Wellness

Whole-Person Approach: Approach wellness holistically, considering all aspects of your life, including physical health, mental health, social connections, and personal development. Strive for balance across these areas to support overall well-being.
Integrated Practices: Integrate wellness practices into your daily routines in a way that feels natural and sustainable. Whether it's a morning meditation, a mid-day walk, or an evening gratitude journal, find practices that fit seamlessly into your life.

2. Prioritize Balance

Work-Life Balance: Maintain a healthy work-life balance by setting clear boundaries between work, personal time, and social media use. Ensure that each area of your life receives appropriate attention and energy.

Recreation and Rest: Make time for recreation and rest, recognizing their importance in maintaining mental wellness. Engage in activities that bring joy, relaxation, and fulfillment, and ensure you get adequate rest and recovery.

Sustaining Mental Wellness and Healthy Social Media Use

Maintaining mental wellness and healthy social media use is an ongoing journey that requires continuous effort, reflection, and adaptation. The strategies outlined in this plan provide a comprehensive approach to achieving balance and resilience in a digital world.

1. Integrate Practices: Embed mental wellness practices into your daily life and adapt them as needed. Regular self-care, mindfulness, and resilience-building are key components.
2. Monitor and Adapt: Regularly assess your progress, adjust your goals, and refine your strategies to align with changing circumstances and needs.
3. Build Support Systems: Develop and nurture supportive relationships and communities that encourage your well-being and provide accountability.

4. Curate Digital Engagement: Practice mindful digital consumption, focusing on content and interactions that contribute positively to your well-being.

5. Leverage Technology: Use technology to support your mental wellness while being mindful of its impact on your digital habits and privacy.

6. Prioritize Balance: Foster a balanced lifestyle that integrates physical health, mental wellness, social connections, and personal development.

By committing to these long-term strategies, you can sustain progress in improving mental wellness and managing social media use effectively. Remember that the journey is unique to each individual, and finding what works best for you will involve ongoing exploration, learning, and adaptation.

Empowering Women: A Journey to Mental Wellness and Social Media

Empowering women through mental wellness and mindful social media use is an ongoing journey that intersects the digital world with the deeply personal realm of mental health. This journey necessitates understanding the unique mental health challenges women face, the profound impact of social media, and the strategies necessary for fostering resilience and well-being.

In modern society, the prevalence of mental health issues among women underscores the urgent need for tailored approaches. Women navigate a complex landscape of biological, social, and cultural pressures, including hormonal changes, gender roles, and societal expectations, all of which contribute to their mental health challenges. Historical contexts have often compounded these difficulties, with long-standing stigmas and stereotypes minimizing women's struggles and access to support. Social media, a dominant force in contemporary life, adds another layer to this complexity. While it offers significant benefits such as connectivity, community building, and access to information, it also presents risks, including cyberbullying, body image concerns, and addictive use. Thus, navigating social media effectively is crucial for women's mental wellness. To empower women, it is essential to adopt holistic and integrated strategies that address both mental wellness and social media management. Building resilience through coping mechanisms, prioritizing self-care, and practicing mindfulness are foundational steps in managing stress and anxiety. Concurrently, setting boundaries around social media use, promoting positive digital interactions, and leveraging the power of community can enhance the positive aspects of digital engagement.

Empowerment through mental wellness and social media management is a multidimensional endeavor that requires continuous learning, adaptation, and community support. By fostering a balanced and mindful approach to both areas, women can achieve greater well-being and navigate the challenges of the digital age more effectively.

The Power of Community: Building Support Networks Through Social Media

The potential of community, especially in the digital age, cannot be overstated. Social media, while often criticized for its negative impacts, holds immense promise as a tool for building supportive networks and fostering positive mental health outcomes.

1. The Nature of Digital Communities

Digital communities transcend geographical boundaries, bringing together individuals with shared interests, experiences, or goals. For women, these communities can provide a sense of belonging, validation, and support that might be lacking in their immediate offline environments. Through groups, forums, and social platforms, women can connect with others who understand their struggles, share their interests, or offer support.

2. Peer Support and Shared Experiences

One of the most significant benefits of online communities is peer support. Women facing mental health challenges can find solace in knowing they are not alone. Sharing personal experiences, challenges, and coping strategies in a supportive environment can reduce feelings of isolation and foster a sense of solidarity. Peer support groups for issues such as anxiety, depression, or postpartum challenges can provide practical advice and emotional support.

3. Access to Resources and Information

Social media platforms and online communities are valuable sources of information and resources related to mental health. Women can access articles, videos, webinars, and expert advice on a wide range of topics, from stress management techniques to self-care practices. This democratization of information empowers women to take control of their mental wellness and make informed decisions about their health.

4. Advocacy and Awareness

Online communities can be powerful advocates for mental health awareness and policy change. Through collective action, social media campaigns, and advocacy groups, women can raise awareness about mental health issues, challenge stigmas, and push for changes in mental health care and support. These efforts contribute to a broader societal understanding and acceptance of mental health needs.

5. Building Personal Networks

Social media enables the formation of personal support networks that extend beyond formal communities. Women can build connections with friends, family, and like-minded individuals who offer encouragement, empathy, and practical support. These personal networks can provide a crucial safety net during difficult times and enhance overall well-being.

6. Cultivating Positive Digital Spaces

Creating and participating in positive digital spaces is key to leveraging the power of community. Women can contribute to a culture of kindness, empathy, and support by sharing positive content, engaging constructively in discussions, and offering encouragement to others. Moderating online groups and fostering inclusive and respectful environments also help build communities that promote mental wellness.

7. Challenges and Considerations

While digital communities offer significant benefits, they also present challenges. Ensuring privacy and managing online conflicts or negativity are important considerations. Women should be mindful of their digital footprint and participate in communities that prioritize safety, respect, and support. Developing digital literacy and critical thinking skills can help navigate these challenges effectively.

In summary, the power of community in the digital age lies in its ability to connect, support, and empower women. By building and participating in supportive networks, women can enhance their mental wellness, advocate for change, and foster positive digital environments that contribute to overall well-being.

The Future of Mental Health: How Social Media Can Be a Tool for Good

Looking forward, the future of mental health is increasingly intertwined with the evolution of social media. Harnessing social media as a tool for good involves recognizing its potential to support mental wellness, advocating for responsible use, and leveraging technological advancements to enhance mental health care.

1. Technological Integration and Innovation

Advances in technology offer new possibilities for integrating mental health support with social media. Innovative solutions, such as mental health apps, virtual support groups, and AI-driven tools, can be seamlessly integrated into social media platforms to provide real-time support and resources. Features such as mood tracking, virtual therapy sessions, and digital well-being analytics can empower users to monitor and improve their mental health effectively.

2. Personalized Mental Health Resources

Social media platforms can leverage algorithms and data analytics to provide personalized mental health resources and recommendations. By analyzing user interactions and preferences, platforms can offer tailored content, such as articles, videos, or support groups, that align with individual needs and interests. Personalization enhances the relevance and impact of the resources provided, making mental health support more accessible and effective.

3. Expanding Access to Care

Social media can play a crucial role in expanding access to mental health care, particularly in underserved or remote areas. Telehealth services and virtual counseling sessions can be facilitated through social media platforms, connecting individuals with mental health professionals regardless of geographical location. This democratization of care ensures that more people have access to the support they need, breaking down barriers related to distance or availability of services.

4. Promoting Mental Health Literacy

Social media can be a powerful tool for promoting mental health literacy and education. Platforms can host campaigns, webinars, and interactive content that educate users about mental health topics, stigma reduction, and self-care practices. By raising awareness and providing accurate information, social media can empower individuals to make informed decisions about their mental health and seek help when needed.

5. Fostering Positive Digital Behavior

Encouraging positive digital behavior is essential for leveraging social media as a tool for good. Platforms can implement features that promote digital well-being, such as screen time management tools, notifications for breaks, and content moderation guidelines. Additionally, promoting positive interactions and discouraging harmful behaviors like cyberbullying can create healthier online environments that support mental wellness.

6. Advocacy and Policy Development

Social media platforms can serve as powerful platforms for advocacy and policy development related to mental health. By amplifying the voices of individuals and organizations advocating for mental health awareness and reform, social media can influence public opinion and drive policy changes. Campaigns for mental health funding, anti-stigma initiatives, and improved access to care can gain momentum through coordinated efforts on social media.

7. Ethical Considerations and Safeguards

As social media becomes more integrated with mental health support, ethical considerations must be addressed. Ensuring user privacy, data security, and the responsible use of algorithms are critical to protecting users' mental health and well-being. Platforms should implement safeguards and transparency measures to maintain trust and ensure that mental health support is provided ethically and responsibly.

8. Community-Driven Innovations

The future of mental health on social media will also be shaped by community-driven innovations. User-generated content, peer support networks, and grassroots movements can drive the development of new approaches and solutions for mental health care. Empowering individuals and communities to contribute to mental health initiatives fosters a collaborative and inclusive approach to addressing mental wellness in the digital age.

Conclusion

As we conclude this journey, it is crucial to acknowledge the profound impact that social media can have on women's mental wellness. The constant barrage of curated perfection, the pressure to conform to societal standards, and the relentless scrutiny can be overwhelming. However, it is not impossible to break free from these shackles and forge a path towards a more authentic and fulfilling life.

The key lies in recognizing the power that lies within each woman. By embracing her unique strengths, passions, and experiences, she can create a sense of purpose and belonging that transcends the superficiality of social media. This journey is not about conforming to societal norms but about embracing individuality and celebrating the beauty of diversity.

To achieve this, women must first acknowledge the importance of self-care and prioritize their mental wellness. This involves setting boundaries, practicing mindfulness, and cultivating a support network of like-minded individuals who share similar values and goals. By doing so, they can create a sense of community and belonging that is not dependent on the fleeting validation of social media.

Moreover, women must also learn to navigate the complexities of social media in a way that promotes their mental wellness. This involves being mindful of the content they consume, the people they follow, and the messages they send. By doing so, they can create a digital environment that is conducive to their well-being and fosters a sense of connection and community.

Ultimately, the journey to mental wellness and social media is not a destination but a continuous process. It requires ongoing effort, self-reflection, and a willingness to adapt and evolve. By embracing this journey, women can break free from the shackles of societal expectations and forge a path towards a more authentic and fulfilling life.

In essence, empowering women to prioritize their mental wellness and navigate social media in a healthy way is crucial for their overall well-being. By embracing individuality, prioritizing self-care, and creating a supportive community, women can break free from the constraints of societal expectations and forge a path towards a more authentic